A LIFE

OF

WASHINGTON

KENNIKAT AMERICAN BICENTENNIAL SERIES

Under the General Editorial Supervision of
Dr. Ralph Adams Brown
Professor of History, State University of New York

Drawn by J.G.Chapman. from the Original bust by Cerracci. Eng'd by J.F.E.Prudhomme.

Washington

HARPER & BROTHERS.

A LIFE

OF

WASHINGTON.

BY

JAMES K. PAULDING.

In Two Volumes.

VOL. I.

HERE
on the 11ᵗʰ February, 1732,
GEO. WASHINGTON
was born.

KENNIKAT PRESS
Port Washington, N. Y./London

A LIFE OF WASHINGTON

First published in 1858
Reissued in 1970 by Kennikat Press
Library of Congress Catalog Card No: 78-120890
ISBN 0-8046-1283-8

Manufactured in the United States of America

KENNIKAT AMERICAN BICENTENNIAL SERIES

PREFACE.

SHORTLY after the conclusion of the late war, the author of the following work removed to the city of Washington, where he resided several years. His situation brought him into familiar intercourse with many respectable, and some distinguished persons, who had been associated with Washington ; and the idea occurred to him of attempting to compile a Life of the Father of his Country, which might possibly address itself to the popular feeling more directly than any one hitherto attempted. With this object in view, he took every occasion to gather information concerning his private life and domestic habits from such sources as could be relied on as authentic.

Though the work has been long delayed, the design has never been relinquished. But subsequent reflection has induced him to alter his original intention, by attempting to adapt it to the use of schools, and generally to that class of readers who have neither the means of purchasing, nor the leisure to read, a larger and more expensive book. It appeared to him, that the life of Washington furnished an invaluable moral example to the youth of his country, and that its introduction to their notice could not but be useful to the rising generation of his countrymen, by holding up to their view the character and actions of a man whose public and private virtues equally furnish the noblest as well as the safest objects for their guide and imitation.

In compiling this work, the writer has availed himself of all the sources of information within his reach ; and though possessed of materials for a much larger one, has compressed them in a man ner which, it is hoped, will bring it within the reach of those to whom it is peculiarly addressed. Much of the information concerning the private life and habits of Washington, was derived from the information of his contemporaries then living, but most of them now no more, and from the means afforded by the present most estimable lady who is now in possession of Mount Vernon.

In detailing the events of the Revolution, the writer has principally consulted the public and private letters of Washington, which have long been before the world, as the most unquestionable authorities ; though it must be obvious, that a work intended for the purposes he has avowed, must necessarily be confined to those more consequential events, in which Washington was himself personally engaged, except in so far as is necessary to connect the narrative. He has avoided citing his authority on every occasion, because such a course would, he thought, interfere with the uses for which the work was intended, by presenting continual interruptions; but his readers may be assured, that he has inserted nothing which he does not believe to be true, and for which, if necessary, he cannot produce the authority of history, of Washington himself, or of undoubted traditions.

In a work addressed to the youth, and to the popular feeling of his country, it seemed allowable, if not absolutely necessary to the purposes of the writer, to place the actions of Washington before the reader in a manner the more strongly to affect his reason as well as his imagination, and to accompany them with reflections calculated to impress him deeply with the virtues and services of the Father of his Country. His desire was to enlist their affections—to call forth their love, as well as veneration, for the great and good man whose life and actions he has attempted to delineate; and in so doing he has appealed rather to the feelings of nature than to the judgment of criticism.

New-York, August, 1835.

CONTENTS

OF

THE FIRST VOLUME.

CHAPTER I.

CHAPTER II.

CHAPTER III.

CHAPTER IV.

CHAPTER V.

CHAPTER VI.

CHAPTER VII.

CHAPTER VIII.

CHAPTER IX.

CHAPTER X.

CHAPTER XI.

LIFE

OF

WASHINGTON.

CHAPTER I.

THERE is no legacy more precious to youth than memorials of great and virtuous men; nor is there any thing which confers more lasting renown on a nation, than the fortunate circum-stance of having produced a citizen whose rare virtues and illustrious actions unite the suffrages of mankind in all ages in his favour, and consecrate him as one of the chosen models of the human race. His country and his countrymen equally partake in the benefits of his services and the glory of his actions; nor is there one of his fellow-citizens throughout all posterity, however humble may be his station, that will not in some degree be ennobled by an association with his name. He becomes the great landmark of his country; the pillar on which is recorded her claim to an equality with the illustrious nations of the world; the example to all succeeding generations: and there is no trait which so strongly marks a degenerate race as an indifference to his fame and his virtues.

Such was the man whose life I have undertaken to write; not because it has not already been well written, or that his renown requires the aid of the historian or biographer. While these record his virtues and his services, they can do little to perpetuate his fame, which is inseparable from his native land. He who, by the general suffrage of his fellow-citizens, is hailed as the FATHER OF HIS COUNTRY, needs no other monument. His memory will last as long as the country endures, and the name of Washington be coexistent with that of the land he redeemed from bondage.

Not for *his* sake, therefore, but for the youth of my country have I commenced this undertaking. I wished, if possible, to place before our children the character and actions of one, the contemplation of whose virtues and services cannot but inspire them with noble sentiments, and a high regard to their public and private duties. In no age or country has there ever arisen a man who, equally in private as in public life, presented so admirable a model to every class and condition of mankind. The most humble citizen of the United States may copy his private virtues, and the most lofty and magnanimous spirit cannot propose to itself a more noble object of ambition than to aspire to an imitation of his public services. In contemplating such a character, our children will equally acquire a reverence for virtue, and a sacred devotion to the obligations of citizens of a free state.

GEORGE WASHINGTON was born in the parish

of Washington,* county of Westmoreland, and
state of Virginia, the twenty-second of Feb
ruary, 1732, and was the youngest son of Augustin Washington and Mary Ball, his second
wife.   He descended from John Washington,
a native of England, who emigrated to this
country sometime between the years 1650 and
1656, and settled at Pope's Creek, where he
married a daughter of the gentleman from
whom the stream derives its name.

Although it is of little consequence who were
the distant ancestors of a man who, by common consent, is hailed as the Father of his
Country, yet any particulars concerning his
family cannot but be a subject of curiosity.   In
all my general reading I have only chanced to
meet with the name of Washington three or
four times in the early history and literature of
England.   In the diary of Elias Ashmole,
founder of the Ashmolean Museum, are the
following entries :—

"*June 12th,* 1645. I entered on my command
as comptroller of the ordnance."

* The first Washington describes himself in his will as "John
Washington, of the parish of Washington."   It is dated Oct. 21,
1675.

"*June* 18*th*. I received my commission from Colonel Washington."

Hume, in his account of the siege of Bristol, has the following passage :—"One party led by Lord Grandison was beaten off and its commander himself mortally wounded. Another, conducted by Colonel Bellasis, met with a like fate. But Washington, with a less party, finding a place in the curtain weaker than the rest, broke in, and quickly made room for the horse to follow." This was in 1643. Five years afterwards, that deluded monarch, Charles I., suffered the just consequences of his offences against the majesty of the people of England, and from that time the cause of royalty appeared desperate. The more distinguished and obnoxious adherents of the Stuarts exiled themselves in foreign lands, and the date of the supposed arrival of the first Washington in Virginia, accords well with the supposition that he may have been the same person mentioned by Ashmole and Hume. In an old collection of poetry, by Sir John Menzies and others, there is a fine copy of verses to the memory of Mr. Washington, page to the king, who died in Spain. In

the year 1640, William Legge, Earl of Dart
mouth, married Elizabeth, daughter of Sir Wil
liam Washington.   But the name and family of
Washington are now extinct in the land of our
forefathers.   When General Washington was
about making his will, he caused inquiries to
be instituted, being desirous to leave some me-
morial to all his relations.   The result was a
conviction that none of the family existed in
that country.   But the topic is rather curious
than important.   The subject of this biography
could receive little additional dignity through a
descent from the most illustrious families of
Christendom.   He stands alone in the pure at-
mosphere of his own glory.   He derived no
title to honours from his ancestry, and left no
child but his country to inherit his fame.

   The house in which Washington was born
stood about half a mile from the junction of
Pope's Creek with the Potomac, and was either
burned or pulled down long previous to the Revolution.   A few scanty relics alone remain to mark
the spot which will ever be sacred in the eyes
of posterity.   A clump of old decayed fig trees,
probably coeval with the mansion, yet exists;
a number of vines, and shrubs, and flowers

still reproduce themselves every year as if to mark its site, and flourish among the hallowed ruins ; and a stone, placed there by Mr. George Washington Custis, bears the simple inscription, "Here, on the 11th of February," (O.S.) "1732, George Washington was born."

The spot is of the deepest interest, not only from its associations, but its natural beauties. It commands a view of the Maryland shore of the Potomac, one of the most majestic of rivers, and of its course for many miles towards Chesapeake Bay. An aged gentleman, still living in the neighbourhood, remembers the house in which Washington was born. It was a low-pitched, single-storied, frame building, with four rooms on the first floor and an enormous chimney at each end on the outside. This was the style of the better sort of houses in those days, and they are still occasionally seen in the old settlements of Virginia.

Such is a brief sketch of the birthplace of a man who was destined to carry to a successful issue those great principles of liberty, which, after having resulted in a degree of happiness and prosperity hitherto unparalleled in the history of mankind, are now spreading afar into the remote regions of the earth, and seem fated to work a universal revolution. Let my young readers bear in mind that it was not in a palace, in the midst of the splendours of royalty, that a child was born, with whose first breath the future destinies of millions of the human race were to be inseparably associated, and whose virtues were to redeem his country from a long-continued vassalage. It was in the house of a private man, like that they themselves inhabit, he first saw the light; and it was by the aid alone of such advantages as are within the reach of them all, that he qualified himself, not only to become the future father of his country, but to exhibit to the world one of the purest models of private excellence, that the history of nations presents to the imitation of mankind. The contemplation of such an illustrious example, will go far to dissolve those long-cherished delusions, created and fostered by early impressions, and the almost universal tendency of books, which have implanted in their minds a conviction that rank, and birth, and wealth, and power are indispensable requisites to great virtues and glorious actions.

The aged neighbour and cotemporary of

Washington, from whom I have derived the preceding description of the house of his nativity, remembers to have heard that at the time of his birth he was very large; and the uniform testimony of those who knew him proves, that in his youth, manhood, and even his declining years, he was distinguished, not only for his vigour, activity, and hardihood, but for an adventurous, resolute, and ardent spirit. His father, Augustin Washington, died when he was scarcely ten years old, leaving him to the care of his mother, who survived a long time, and lived to see her favourite son hailed by a grateful people as their deliverer.

But young as was Washington at the decease of his father, it is stated, on the authority of the rector of the parish of Mount Vernon, that he lived long enough to implant in his heart the seeds of virtuous principles, which, falling on a rich soil, grew up in time to a glorious maturity. The virtues of truth, justice, and liberality, most especially, were early impressed on his youthful mind, by examples and illustrations, and the principles of religion inculcated with his earliest lessons. From all that is remembered of Augustin Washington, he appears to have been a good man, worthy of such a son.

The mother of Washington, on whom the care of bringing him up devolved on the death of his father, is described to me, by those who knew her well, as a woman of ordinary stature, once a great belle and beauty in that part of Virginia called the Northern Neck. High-spirited, yet of great simplicity of manners, uncommon strength of mind, and decision of character, she exacted great deference from her sons, of whom George was the favourite. The only weakness in her character was an excessive fear of thunder, which originated in the melancholy death of a young female friend, who was struck dead at her side by lightning, when Mrs. Washington was about fifteen years old.

The same inflexible regard to the performance of those ordinary duties of life, on which so much of our own happiness and that of others depends; the same strict punctuality in keeping her word, and discharging all the obligations of justice, by which Washington was distinguished, characterized his mother. There was a plain honesty and truth about her, peculiar to that age, and which has been ill exchanged for empty professions and outward polish. As a native of Virginia, she was hospitable by birthright, and always received her visiters with a smiling welcome. But they were never asked to stay but once, and she always speeded the parting guest, by affording every facility in her power. She possessed all those domestic habits and qualities that confer value on women, but had no desire to be distinguished by any other titles than those of a good wife and mother. She was once present, and occupied the seat of honour, at a ball given to Washington at Fredericksburg, while in the full measure of his well-earned glory, and when nine o'clock came, said to him with perfect simplicity, "Come, George, it is time to go home."

Though the early years of Washington are shrouded in the mists of time, I have been enabled, through the kindness of one, whose modest and retiring dignity would scarcely forgive me were I to mention her name, to communicate some interesting particulars of his course of domestic discipline. It will appear from these, that the loss of one parent was amply supplied by the well-directed cares of another, and that he derived his character from the purest fountains of piety and wisdom.

I have now before me a venerable volume, printed in the year 1685, entitled, " Contemplations, Moral and Divine, by Sir Matthew Hale, ate Chief-justice of the Court of King's-Bench," in which is written, with her own hand, the name of " Mary Washington." It bears the appearance of frequent use, and particular chapters are designated by marks of reference. It is the volume from which the mother of Washington was accustomed to read daily lessons of piety, morality, and wisdom to her children. The value of such a relic cannot be better set forth than in the language which accompanied its transmission; and I can only devoutly hope that the hallowed sanctuary of Mount Vernon may ever continue to be possessed by such kindred spirits as the writer of that letter.

" I beg it may be carefully preserved and returned, as one of the family heirlooms which better feelings than pride would retain for future generations to look on, even should they not study it. There is something in a reverence for religion favourable to a virtuous character; and that reverence is in some measure kept alive by looking on a family Bible, and solid works of divinity, which have descended from past generations. We associate with them recollections of ancestral virtues, and when family tradition assures us they were the counsellors of past days, there is a feeling of the heart which turns to them in time of trial, and makes it good, I think, to leave them an honourable station, as friends to those that have gone before, and those who shall come after us, to speak in the cause of truth when we shall sleep in the grave."

I shall make some extracts from such portions of this book as appear to have been most used, not only because they contain the finest lessons of piety, morality, and wisdom, but most especially because I think the germ of Washington's character may be traced in the principles and practice they so eloquently inculcate. One of the chapters which appears to have been selected as an ordinary lesson, and marked for that purpose in the table of contents, is denominated "The Great Audit, and seems to me to contain as much true wisdom as was ever imbodied in the same compass. I shall extract those parts which most singularly assimilate with the character of Washington, in order that my youthful readers may see whence it was that, in all probability, the Father of his Country derived his principles of action, and, if possible, imitate his virtues.

"As touching my conscience, and the light thou hast given me in it, I have been very jealous of wounding, or grieving, or discouraging, or deadening it. I have therefore chosen rather to foster that which seemed but indifferent, lest there should be somewhat in it that might be useful; and would rather gratify my conscience with being too scrupulous than displease or disquiet it by being too venturous. I have still chosen, therefore, what might be probably lawful, than to do what might possibly be unlawful; because, though I could not err in the former, I might in the latter. If things were disputable, whether they might be done, I rather chose to forbear, because the lawfulness of my forbearance was unquestionable.

"Touching human prudence and understanding in affairs, and dexterity in the arranging of them: I have ever been careful to mingle justice and honesty with my prudence, and have always esteemed prudence, actuated by injustice and falsity, the arrantest and most devilish practice in the world, because it prostitutes thy gift to the service of hell, and mingles a beam of thy divine excellence with an extract of the devil's furnishing, making a man so much the worse by how much he is wiser than others.

"I always thought that wisdom which, in a tradesman or a politician, was mingled with deceit, falsity, and injustice, deserved the same name, only the latter is so much the worse, because it is of the more public and general concernment. Yet because I have often observed great employments, especially in public affairs, are sometimes under great temptations of mingling too much craft with prudence, and then to miscall it policy, I have, as much as may be, avoided such temptations, and if I have met with them, I have resolutely rejected them.

"I have always observed that honesty and plain-dealing in transactions, as well public as private, is the best and soundest prudence and policy, and commonly, at the long-run, over-matcheth craft and subtilty. And more advantage is derived from possessing the confidence of mankind, than can ever be made by deceiving them.

"As human prudence is abused if mingled with falsity and deceit, though the end be ever so good, so it is much more debased if directed to a bad end, to the dishonour of thy name, the oppression of thy people, the corrupting thy worship or truth, or to practise any injustice towards any person.

"It hath been my care as not to err in the manner, so neither in the end of the exercising of thy providence. I have ever esteemed thy prudence best employed when it was exercised in the preservation and support of thy truth, in contemning, discovering, and disappointing the designs of evil and treacherous men, in delivering the oppressed, in righting the injured, in preventing of wars and discords, in preserving the public peace and tranquillity of the people where I live, and in all those offices laid upon me by thy providence, under every relation.

"When my end was most unquestionably

good, I ever then took most heed that the means were suitable and justifiable. Because the better the end was, the more easily are we cozened into the use of ill means to effect it. We are too apt to dispense with ourselves in the practice of what is amiss, in order to the accomplishment of an end that is good ; we are apt, while with great intenseness of mind we gaze upon the end, not to take care what course we take so we attain it; and we are apt to think that God will dispense with, or at least overlook the miscarriages in our attempts, if the end be good.

" Because many times, if not most times, thy name and honour do more suffer by attempting a good end by bad means, than by attempting both a bad end, and by bad means. For bad ends are suitable to bad means; they are alike —and it doth not immediately as such concern thy honour. But every thing that is good hath somewhat of thee in it, thy name, and thy nature, and thy honour is written upon it; and the blemish that is cast upon it, is, in some measure, cast upon thee. The evil, and scan dal, and ugliness that is in the means, is cast upon the end, and doth disparage and blemish it, and, consequently, is dishonour to thee. To rob for burnt-offerings, or to lie for God, is a greater disservice to thy majesty, than to rob for rapine, or to lie for advantage."

"Touching my eminence of place and power in this world, this is my account. I never sought or desired it, and that for these reasons. First, because I easily saw that it was rather a burden than a privilege. It made my charge and my account the greater, my contentment and my rest the less. I found enough in it to make me decline it in respect to myself, but not any that could invite me to seek or desire it.

"That external glory and splendour that attended it I esteemed as vain and frivolous in itself, a bait to allure vain and inconsiderate persons to affect and delight—not valuable enough to invite a considerate judgment to desire or undertake it. I esteemed them as the gilding that covers a bitter pill, and I looked through this dress and outside and easily saw that it covered a state obnoxious to danger, solicitude, care, trouble, envy, discontent, unquietness, temptation, and vexation.

"I esteemed it a condition which, if there

were any distempers abroad, they would be infallibly hunting and pushing at it; and if it found any corruptions within, either of pride, vainglory, insolence, vindictiveness, or the like, it would be sure to draw them out and set them to work. And if they prevailed, it made my power and greatness not only my burden but my sin; if they prevailed not, yet it required a most watchful, assiduous, and severe labour and industry to suppress them.

"When I undertook any place of power or eminence, first, I looked to my call thereunto to be such as I might discern to be thy call, not my own ambition. Second, that the place was such as might be answered by suitable abilities in some measure to perform. Third, that my end in it might not be the satisfaction of any pride, ambition, or vanity in myself, but to serve Providence and my generation honestly and faithfully.

"In the holding or exercising these places, I kept my heart humble; I valued not myself one rush the more for it. First, because I easily found that that base affectation of pride, which commonly is the fly that haunts such employments, would render me dishonourable to thy majesty, and discreditable in the employment. Second, because I easily saw that great places were slippery places, the mark of envy. It was, therefore, always my care so to behave in them as I might be in a capacity to leave them; and so to leave them, as that, when I had left them, I might have no scars and blemishes stick upon me. I carried, therefore, the same evenness of temper in holding them as might become me if I were without them. I found enough in great employments to make me sensible of the danger, trouble, and cares of them; enough to make me humble, but not enough to make me proud and haughty.

"I never made use of my power or greatness to serve my own turns, either to heap up riches, or oppress my neighbour, or to revenge injuries, or to uphold injustice. For, though others thought me great, I knew myself to be still the same, and in all things, besides the due execution of my place, my deportment was just the same as if I had been no such man; for I very well and practically knew that place, and honour, and preferment are things extrinsical, and have no ingredience into the man.

His value and estimate before, and under, and after his greatness is still the same in itself— as the counter that now stands for a penny, anon for sixpence, and anon for twelve pence is still the same counter, though its place and extrinsical denomination be changed."

"Though I have loved my reputation, and have been careful not to lose or impair it by my own neglect, yet I have looked upon it as a brittle thing that the devil aims to hit in an especial manner; a thing that is much in the power of a false report, a mistake, or misapprehension to wound and hurt, and notwithstanding all my care, I am at the mercy of others, without God's wonderful overruling providence.

"And as my reputation is the esteem that others have of me, so that esteem may be blemished without my default. I have, therefore, always taken this care not to set my heart upon my reputation. I will use all fidelity and honesty, and take care it shall not be lost by any default of mine, and if, notwithstanding all this, my reputation be foiled by evil or man, I will patiently bear it, and content myself with the serenity of my own conscience.

"When thy honour or the good of my country was concerned, I then thought it was a seasonable time to lay out my reputation for the advantage of either, and to act with it, and by it, and upon it, to the highest, in the use of all lawful means. And upon such an occasion, the counsel of Mordecai to Esther was my encouragement,—'*Who knoweth whether God hath not given thee this reputation and esteem for such a time as this?*'"

This admirable book is filled with lessons of virtue and wisdom, clothed in the simple language of sincerity and truth, and adorned in its hoary dignity, like some ancient temple, with rich vines, bearing clusters of flowers, and beautiful even in its decay. It has evidently been much used, and especially in those passages containing enforcements and exemplifications of the higher duties of men. It is the work of a pious and venerable sage, whose whole life illustrated his own precepts, and without doubt contributed much to form the character of the man who scarcely conferred greater benefits on his country by his actions than posterity will derive from his example.

From this indissoluble connection between good precepts imbibed in early youth, and good actions performed in manhood and old age, the children of America may learn the value of a virtuous education, and make a proper use of those opportunities which the affection of parents and the munificence of their country afford them. These are among the rich gifts, the "talents," bestowed upon them by the Giver of all good, and according as they use them well or ill will they be able to answer when called upon at the "great audit," when the trumpet shall sound, and the graves give up their dead.

There is little reason to doubt that much of the education of Washington was domestic; that education which, more than all the rest, shapes the course and the character of the future man. This generally falls to the mother, and it is from the source whence children draw their life, that they for the most part derive those qualities and virtues which alone make life valuable to others and to themselves. A firm, tender, careful, and sensible mother is the greatest blessing that ever fell to the lot of a human being. It is from her that the young shoot derives its bent; it is from her it receives its nurture and its cultivation, and it is to her that the children of men should in after life look up as the fountain of benefits which a whole life of grateful duty can scarcely repay. Such a mother had Washington, and such was her reward.

The estate at Pope's Creek, as appears from the will of John Washington, a copy of which is in my possession, having been left to Lawrence Washington, the father of George removed to another, situated on the river Rappahannock, in Stafford county, near Fredericksburg. After his death, however, though I cannot determine precisely at what age, he was sent down into Westmoreland to his half-brother, Augustin, where he attended the school of a Mr. Williams, said to have been an excellent teacher. Previous to his removal from his native place, he had received his first rudiments at a school kept by a man of the name of Hobby, a tenant of his father, who, it is stated, officiated as sexton and gravedigger to the parish of Washington. The same authority says that Hobby lived to see his illustrious pupil riding on the full tide of his glory, and was wont to boast that he " had laid the foundation of his greatness."

At the school of Mr. Williams, he maintained that standing among boys which he was destined to sustain among men. Such was his character for veracity that his word was sufficient to settle a disputed point with the scholars, who were accustomed to receive his award with acclamations ; and such his reputation for courage as well as firmness, that though he never on any occasion fought with his fellows, he never received either insult or wrong. He was as much beloved as respected, and when he left school, it is said that the scholars parted from him with tears.

From traditionary information which I rely on, it also appears that at a very early age Washington gave indications of a military spirit, which is, however, so generally a characteristic of boys, that it can scarcely be said to distinguish one from another. He inherited from his father great strength and activity, and was accustomed, not only at school, but long afterwards, to practise the most athletic exercises. Thus it was that he prepared himself to encounter the fatigues and hardships of his future life.

Five years after the death of his father, and, consequently, when under fifteen years of age, he left school for the last time. What were the acquisitions he carried with him cannot now be known. They were certainly confined to the ordinary branches of an English education, at a period when knowledge and the means of acquiring it in this country were not what they are now. A great portion of the youth of the colonies of any peculiar claims to distinction were sent abroad for their education; the good people of that period seeming to have cherished a conviction that knowledge and learning could never be naturalized in the New World.

While it serves to exalt the character and abilities of this famous man, to learn that though his means of acquiring knowledge were not superior, nay, not equal, to those now within the reach of all for whom I write, yet did he in after life by the force of his genius and the exercise of a manly perseverance, supply all his deficiencies; so that when called upon to take charge of the destinies of his country, and bear a load as heavy as was ever laid on the shoulders of man, he was found gloriously adequate to the task, and bore her triumphantly through a struggle which may be likened to the agonies of death resulting in immortality. As with him, so with my youthful readers, most of whose opportunities of acquiring knowledge are greater than those of Washington, and who, though they will never reach his fame, may still rationally aspire to an imitation of his perseverance, his integrity, and his patriotism. Opportunities for great actions occur but seldom, but every day and every hour presents occasion for the performance of our duties.

Fortunately, perhaps, for Washington, he was not born rich. The property of his father was large, but it was to be shared among several children. Thus was he early in life led to look for fortune and consequence to that best of all sources, his own talents and exertions. From the period of his leaving the school in Westmoreland until old enough to engage in the active business of life, he resided either with his mother at the plantation on the Rappahannock, or with his half-brother, Lawrence Washington, at Mount Vernon. His leisure hours, it appears, were spent in athletic exercises, in which he excelled; most especially in running, wrestling, and riding, in all of which, those who recollect him at that time agree in saying, he was greatly distinguished. Such was his skill, grace, and dignity in the latter especially, that during his whole life, he was considered the finest rider in Virginia, where this was a universal accomplishment.

His sports and recreations were, however, at a maturer age, and when his situation demanded it, or when his future prospects stimulated him to the exercise of those talents which he must have been conscious of possessing, mingled with study and reflection. Yet this habit of exercise continued with him through life, and, combined with the vigour and fortitude of his mind, enabled him to sustain without flinching, all those vicissitudes and hardships which it was his destiny and duty to encounter in the cause of his country. It is by the aid of a strong body, a cultivated mind, and virtuous principles, that we are qualified to perform great actions for the benefit of mankind.

George was the favourite son of his mother, yet he was not a spoiled child, as is usual in such cases. The strength and steadiness of his mind, equally with that of Mrs. Washington, preserved him from the evils of early indulgence. The simplicity of her character was combined with firmness and decision. The following anecdote equally illustrates the principles of mother and son, and is derived from an authentic source.

Mrs. Washington was very fond of fine horses, insomuch that when on one occasion she had become possessed of a pair of handsome grays, she caused them to be turned out to pasture in a meadow in front of the house, from whence they could at all times be seen from the window of her sitting-room. It chanced that she at one time owned a favourite young horse, which had never been broke to the saddle, and no one was permitted to ride. On some occasion, a party of youthful Nimrods on a visit to the house, proposed, after dinner, to mount the colt and make the circuit of the pasture. No one could do the feat, and many were defeated in attempting to mount, or thrown from his back afterwards. Washington, then but a youth, succeeded, however, and gave the favourite such a breathing that he at length fell under his rider, who immediately went and told his mother what he had done. Her reply deserves to be recorded. "Young man," said she, "I forgive you, because you have the courage to tell the truth at once ; had you skulked away, I should have despised you."

It is easy to imagine that, acting on these principles, the result should be, on the part of Washington, an inflexible regard to the obliga tions of sincerity and truth. Accordingly, such was the character of this great and virtuous citizen, during the whole course of his noble and exemplary life, in all situations, and under all circumstances. No man, perhaps, ever oc- cupied stations, both in war and peace, more decidedly calculated to draw his frailties before the world, or instigate the bitterest calumnies. Yet he passed through his high career unstained by a single imputation of falsehood, deception, or crime ; the sanctity of his character tri- umphed over the violence of national hostility and party feelings, and he died, as he had lived, with a fame as pure as ever fell to the lot of man.

Such are the few materials I have been able to collect, concerning the first eighteen years of Washington's life. No one probably antici- pated his future eminence, for none could fore-

see that great revolution which has excited the
pulse of the world. None prophesied at that
time that he would one day become the first,
among the first of every age, the great champion of the liberties of mankind, the model of
virtuous heroism, and, consequently, none were
found to preserve or record that portion of the
lives of ordinary men, which does not deserve
to be remembered. Nor perhaps is this omis-
sion to be regretted when we see so many
illustrious persons, who, contemplated in the distance and through the mists of time, assume
the port of giants, dwindle into pigmies, by
having all their pigmy actions placed before
the world. Those heroes always fare best
whose memories are traditionary rather than his-
torical, or whose lives have been written long
after their little peculiarities and weaknesses,
the thousand insignificant nothings that make
up so large a portion of human actions, have
passed into oblivion, and nothing is remembered
but what is intrinsically great. It has hitherto
been found impossible to mar the severe simplicity of Washington's greatness by coupling
it with puerilities that have neither the merit

of illustrating his character, or increasing our stores of useful knowledge.

That he had established a reputation which placed him very early in life above his cotemporaries, can hardly be doubted, when my young readers shall learn that at the age of nineteen he was appointed a deputy Adjutant-General of the State of Virginia, and this, too, at a period when the attention of the government had been turned to the training of her provincial troops, in consequence of the alleged encroachments of the French on the Ohio. Such an appointment, to so young a man, is presumptive evidence that he had thus early attracted notice on the score of some extraordinary qualifications.

Previous to this, however, he had, on a visit to his half-brother Lawrence, become known to Mr. William Fairfax, a near relative of Lord Fairfax, then proprietor of the Northern Neck of Virginia, one of the largest estates that ever fell to the lot of a private individual. A connection had taken place between the Washington and Fairfax families, in consequence of the marriage of Lawrence Washington with a sister of William Fairfax, then a member of the Virginia Council. The latter gentleman introduced Washington to Lord Fairfax, who gave him the appointment of surveyor to his vast estate, in consequence of which he had frequent occasion to explore the uninhabited regions of the back woods, where he became accustomed to a life of exposure, and strengthened his habits and constitution by a series of hardships and exposures. Lord Fairfax lived to hear of Cornwallis laying down his arms to his former surveyor, when, as tradition says, he called for his personal attendant, an old negro, and cried out, "Take me to bed, it is high time for me to die!" It is certain that he never left it till carried to his grave.

The character, habits, and inclinations of Washington were, however, decidedly military. At the age of fourteen he applied for and received a warrant of midshipman in the British navy. Happily for himself, for his country, for the world, the interference and entreaties of his mother induced him to relinquish it very unwillingly, and preserved to the cause of liberty its most illustrious champion. Had it been otherwise, he who became the deliverer of his country might have arrived, perhaps, at the dignity of a post-captain. It seems like an interposition of Providence in behalf of the liberties of mankind. His baggage was already on board a man-of-war riding in the Potomac just below Mount Vernon, when the entreaties of his mother induced him to sacrifice his long-cherished wishes to the duties of a son.

But it seems he did not the less cultivate a knowledge of the theory and practice of war. A certain Adjutant Muse, of the county of Westmoreland, acquainted with military tactics, who had accompanied Lawrence Washington in the expedition against Carthagena, taught George the manual exercise, in which he soon acquired great dexterity. He also borrowed of this person certain treatises on the art of war, by the aid of which he acquired a knowledge, at least, of its theory, and became an expert fencer under the tuition of Monsieur Van Braam, who was subsequently his interpreter in his intercourse with the French on the Ohio. There can be little doubt that it was a knowledge of these acquirements, and of his decided military propensities, that so early pointed him out to the notice of his government The foundation of our future fortunes is laid in the days of our youth; the blossoms when blighted in the spring, never produce the rich fruits of summer and autumn. Had not Washington thus early cultivated his mind and invigorated his body, instead of becoming the sword and shield of freedom, its defender and its mentor, he might have sunk under the weight of his after burthens, and crushed himself with the ruins of his country.

Hitherto I have confined my narrative to the private life and character of Washington. During the period over which we have passed, he was silently preparing himself, by useful studies, active employment, and athletic exercises, for that magnificent career which opened before him vista after vista, by slow and painful labours, until, through a series of disasters and triumphs—of gloomy hopes and bitter disappointments—of long-suffering and keen anxieties—of virtuous sacrifices, unconquerable courage, patience, fortitude, and perseverance, animated by patriotism, and inspired by a genius equal to every emergency, he reached the summit of imperishable fame. I am now to exhibit him to my youthful readers in new and trying situations, where, though but a boy, he became charged with the affairs of men, and the interests of states. It will be found that, like the sun, as he rose in the firmament, he diffused additional light and warmth over a wider circumference.

CHAPTER II.

It is not necessary to discuss the conflicting claims of France and England to the territory of North America. The one has now no possessions left, and the period is probably not far distant when the New World will be entirely emancipated from the dominion of those who, though they can scarcely govern at home, aspire to control the distant regions of the earth. These claims were equally founded on the right of discovery, a right for the most part much more satisfactory to the discoverer than the discovered. It is enough to say, that between these two rival nations, their claims comprehended nearly the whole of this great continent, from the Gulf of Mexico to Hudson's Bay, and from the Atlantic to the uttermost regions of the unexplored west. One might suppose here was enough for both; but experience teaches us that the possession of much is only a prelude to the desire of more; and, accordingly, the two nations began to dispute and ultimately to fight about a wilderness of which neither knew the boundaries or dimensions.

As my design is rather to write the life of Washington than the history of the era in which he flourished, I shall press nothing into the service but what seems necessary to this purpose. It will be sufficient to state that the pretensions of the French interfered with those of the English, and the ancient rivalry of the two nations requiring but a single spark to set both in a flame, hostilities were the natural consequence of their conflicting ambition. The French advanced from one step to another, until at length they reached the Ohio, and subsequently established a post at the junction of the Alleghany and Monongahela rivers, on the spot where Pittsburg now stands The ultimate object of their plans was to confine the English to the country east of the Alleghany mountains, and, of consequence, give the French a decided superiority on this continent.

Virginia was especially interested in these encroachments. Her chartered limits extended quite across from sea to sea, and her frontier lay exposed to the hostilities of the French on the Ohio, aided by the Indians, over whom they always acquired a paramount influence by their religion, their politeness, and their gallantry. These movements on the Ohio of consequence excited great apprehensions in the Ancient Dominion, and preparations were made to meet what might follow by raising and disciplining the provincial militia. The eyes of the state were turned to the valiant spirits of her youthful sons, and the first public station conferred on Washington was that of adjutant-general of Virginia, with the rank of major, when he was scarcely nineteen years of age. But with the ardent vigour of youth he combined the qualities of mature manhood, and the appointment was not only justified by prudence, but by the whole tenor of his after-life.

Lieutenant Governor Dinwiddie, then the representative of royalty in Virginia, became alarmed, and the state more than partook in his apprehensions. At that period, the whole country west of the Alleghanies was one vast wilderness, roamed by wild beasts, and Indians equally savage and wild. The great valley of the Shenandoah, now rich with the labours of thousands and tens of thousands of independent farmers, was then thinly inhabited by white men, who could not see the smoke of their neighbours chimneys; and Winchester was just on the edge of the civilized world towards the west. Often had they suffered from the incursions of bloody and remorseless savages, sparing neither sex nor age, and wreaking their inhuman rage on the breathless bodies after their souls had departed from the scene of suffering. The approach of the French, their probable hostile views, and their known influence over the wild and wayward children of the forest, created the most gloomy anticipations that those scenes, which, as described by the aged settlers to their children, made them shiver and turn pale, would be once more renewed with aggravated horrors.

To avert these dangers, to remonstrate against these encroachments, to obtain information of the feelings cherished by the Indians towards the respective claimants to the empire of the New World, and to conciliate them by every means in his power, Governor Dinwiddie determined to despatch an envoy to St. Pierre, the French commandant on the Ohio. This was no embassy of state, no courtly pageant, where the vanity of man may be gratified by an intercourse with the great. It was a service full of danger and difficulty; it required courage, fortitude, perseverance, and personal vigour, to endure the hardships and perils of the pathless solitudes of nature. Many declined the ungrateful service, and not one of the aids or attendants of the governor was willing to undertake the task. In this crisis, young Washington, before the laws of his country had recognised him as a man, volunteered his services. The governor, a sturdy old Scotsman, accepted the tender, saying, at the same time, "Faith, you're a brave lad, and, if you play your cards well, you shall have no cause to repent your bargain."

Requiring but a single day to make his preparations, he departed into the wide wilderness, accompanied by Van Braam, his old fencing-master, as his interpreter, and two servants, bearing the governor's letter to the French commandant. It was now the middle of autumn, and the forests began to shed their brown leaves, which covered the earth with her autumnal carpet. A sort of military road conducted the party as far as Will's Creek, beyond which a guide was necessary. They arrived there on the fourteenth of November, and the next day, having engaged a guide and four additional attendants, proceeded on their way. Excessive rains, aided by the melting of the snows, had so swelled the streams which crossed their route, that the journey was one of continued labour and difficulty. It was not until the eighth day after their departure from Will's Creek, that they reached the junction of the Alleghany and Monongahela rivers.

Having preceded his attendants and baggage on this occasion, as was always his custom in danger and difficulty, he occupied his time until their arrival in a manner which, as it illustrates the sagacity and foresight of a youth under twenty, is peculiarly worthy the notice of my young readers. I extract the words from the journal of Washington himself, a copy of which is now before me. " As I got down before the canoe, I spent some time in viewing the rivers and land in the fork, which I think extremely well situated for a fort, as it has the absolute command of both rivers. The land at the point is twenty-five feet above the common level of the water, and a considerable bottom of flat well-timbered land all round it, well calculated for building. The rivers are each a quarter of a mile wide, and run here at nearly right angles ; Alleghany bearing north-east, and Monongahela south-east. The former of these is very rapid running water ; the other deep and still, without any perceptible fall." The French, who chose their military positions in this country with a skill and foresight which has ever since been a subject of admiration, soon after erected a fort on this very spot, where has since grown up the great manufacturing city of Pittsburg.

I should here introduce an entire copy of this interesting journal, the earliest production of

Washington on record, did not the design I have in view confine this work within a limited space. For the same reason I shall content myself with detailing a few of the most interesting particulars connected with the expedition He delivered his letter to the French com mandant, and endeavoured to induce the Indian chiefs of the neighbouring tribes to meet him in council, a measure which the commandant used all his efforts to prevent. Finally, he ascertained the views of the French government through M. Joncaire and other officers, who declared, at an entertainment given to Washington, that it was their intention to take possession of the Ohio, which they claimed on the ground of its discovery by the celebrated and unfortunate La Salle.

Having completed the purposes of his mission, so far as was practicable, he prepared to set out on his return. But, by this time, his horses had become too weak to carry the provisions necessary to subsist them in the wilderness. Washington at once determined to proceed on foot to some point where others might be procured. I shall give one more extract from his journal, because it affords a noble example of resolution and hardihood to my youthful readers. The contrast between Washington trudging through the pathless wilderness, with no other garment than his watch-coat, a gun in his hand, and a pack on his shoulders, with Washington at the head of armies, wielding the destiny of a great people, sustaining the inestimable rights of the human race, living the object of the world's admiration, and dying with the sacred name of Father of his Country, is alike striking for its romantic singularity, as for its sublime moral. Virtue, courage, and patriotism, are the three great steps of Jacob's ladder, which lead from earth to heaven.

"I took," he says, "my necessary papers, pulled off my clothes, and tied myself up in a watch-coat. Then, with gun in hand, and pack on my back, in which were my papers and provisions, I set out with Mr. Gist the 26th (of December). The next day, after we had passed a place called Murdering Town, we fell in with a party of French Indians who had lain in wait for us. One of them fired at us, not fifteen steps off, but fortunately missed. We took the fellow into custody, and kept him till nine o'clock at night, then let him go, and walked the remaining part of the night without making any stop, that we might get the start so far as to be out of the reach of pursuit the next day, since we were well assured they would follow our track as soon as it was light. The next day we continued travelling until quite dark, and got to the river about two miles above Shanopin. We expected to have found the river frozen, but it was not, except about fifty yards from the shore. The ice, I suppose, had broken up above, for it was driving in vast quantities.

"There was no way of getting over but on a raft, which we set about with but one poor hatchet, and finished just after sunsetting. This was a whole day's work. We next launched it—then went on board and set off—but before we were half over, we were jammed in the ice in such a manner that we expected every moment our raft to sink, and ourselves to perish. I put out my setting-pole to try and stop the raft, that the ice might pass by, when the rapidity of the stream threw it with such force against the pole, that it jerked me out into ten feet water; but I fortunately saved myself by

catching hold of one of the raft-logs. Notwithstanding all our efforts, we could not get to
either shore, but were obliged, as we were near
an island, to quit our raft and make for it.

"The cold was extremely severe, and Mr.
Gist had all his fingers and some of his toes
frozen. The water was shut up so hard that
we found no difficulty in getting off the island
the next morning on the ice, and proceeding to
Mr. Frazier's. We met here with twenty warriors who were going to the southward to war;
but coming to a place at the head of the Great
Kenawha, where they found seven people
killed and scalped (all but one woman with
light hair), they turned about and ran back, for
fear the inhabitants should rise, and take them
for the authors of the murders. They report
that the bodies were lying about the house, and
some of them torn and eaten by the hogs. As
we intended to take horses here, and it required
some time to find them, I went up three miles
to the Yohogany to visit Queen Allequippa, who
had expressed great concern that we passed
her in going to the fort. I made her a present
of a watch-coat and a bottle of rum, which latter
was thought much the best present of the two."

In the midst of such wild scenes, Indian haunts, and forest adventures, were the first years devoted by Washington to the service of his country passed. It might have been expected that this apprenticeship to savage warfare, this daily experience of bloody massacres and inhuman barbarity, would have aided in making his deportment rough and his disposition ferocious. But it was not so. In the whole course of his after-life he maintained a mild yet dignified courtesy to all mankind, and throughout his long military career not one act of cruelty was ever justly laid to his charge. His piety and his principles placed him above the reach of contamination, and neither adversity nor prosperity could corrupt his mind or influence his manners. The gold was too pure to become rusted by any vicissitudes.

He arrived at Williamsburg, then the seat of government in Virginia, where he waited on the governor, delivered the answer of the French commandant on the Ohio to his letter, and gave an account of his proceedings, which met the entire approbation of that officer. Nor was this all. The House of Burgesses was then in session, and Washington happening to enter the gallery, the speaker immediately rose, and moved that "the thanks of the House be given to Major Washington, who now sits in the gallery, for the gallant manner in which he executed the important trust lately reposed in him by his excellency Governor Dinwiddie." Every member of the House now rose and saluted Washington with a general bow, and the sentiment of the speaker was echoed by more than one member expressing his sense of his merit and services. Washington in vain attempted to make his acknowledgments for this high honour. His voice failed him, and the frame that never before or after trembled in the presence of an enemy, now faltered under the compliments of assembled friends. It was then that the speaker, noticing his unconquerable embarrassment, made him this just and memorable compliment,—"Sit down, Major Washington; your modesty is alone equal to your merit." It will appear in the sequel that this modesty accompanied him through his whole life, and while it acted as a stimulus to new exertions, checked every feeling, or, at least, exhibition, of pride at their success. Though, in all probability aware of his superiority over other men, this consciousness never operated to diminish his ardour to increase it by every means in his power; nor did he ever yield to the common foible of youth, which converts premature honours into .an excuse for a total remission of all future efforts to deserve them.

CHAPTER III.

Washington accompanies his Brother Lawrence to Bermuda.
where he gets the Small-pox—Affection of Lawrence for his
Brother George—He rejoices in his rising reputation, pre
dicts his future Eminence, and, when he dies, leaves him
the Estate at Mount Vernon—Troubles between France and
England—Virginia raises a Regiment—Washington declines
the Command, but accepts the Post of Lieutenant Colonel—
Proceeds to the Great Meadows and builds Fort Necessity—
Succeeds to the Command of the Regiment—Advances towards Fort Duquesne—Retreats to his Fort—Is besieged and
captured—Retires from the Service soon after in Disgust, but
accepts the Post of Volunteer Aid to General Braddock—De
parture for Fort Duquesne.

DURING the interim between his expedition
to the Ohio and his appointment as second in
command of the regiment raised by Virginia to
protect herself against the anticipated hostility
of the French and Indians, Washington accompanied his brother Lawrence in a voyage to Bermuda for the benefit of his health. Lawrence had
a great affection for George, and often pressed

him to reside with him at Mount Vernon. But the young man wisely preferred making his own way in the world by his own exertions, and, as I have before related, accepted the situation of surveyor to the estate of Lord Fairfax.

He, however, yielded to the wishes of his brother, whom he tenderly loved, and accompanied him to Bermuda. He was then wasting away with a consumption, from which he never recovered. While at the island, Washington caught the small-pox, with which he became slightly marked for the remainder of his life. It is traditionary in the family that the brothers never met after George departed on the expedition in which he was finally captured by the French and Indians, as will be related in the sequel. Lawrence, however, often heard of the exploits of his favourite brother, rejoiced in his growing fame, predicted his future eminence, and, when he died, left him the estate at Mount Vernon, since become the shrine of thousands of pilgrims from among his countrymen and distant nations.

In the mean time, the conflicting claims of France and England were coming to a crisis, and that crisis is always war. The news of the alleged encroachments of the former having reached the British ministers, measures were taken for the formation of a confederacy among the colonies, for the purposes of defence or retaliation. As the dangers were mutual, although some were more exposed than others, each was to contribute its proportion to the general defence in case of need. Virginia being the nearest, naturally expected the first blow, and was of course most prompt in preparing for the storm. A regiment was raised, and Washington was placed second to Colonel Fry, who dying shortly after, the command devolved on the former.

In the perusal of this work, my young readers will bear in mind, I trust, that the means used for attaining their ends are not to be judged of by their magnitude, but their consequences Great battles and oceans of bloodshed frequently produce nothing but their inevitable results, misery and despair, while often events and instruments apparently the most insignificant lead to consequences which affect the welfare of millions, and change the relations of the world. This remark is especially applicable to the history of the United States from the first moment of the landing of the pilgrims at Jamestown and Plymouth to the present time Often on the lives of a few wanderers in the interminable wilderness of the west, depended, perhaps, the question whether millions of beings should be now in existence or should never have existed; and often on circumstances, in themselves apparently of no consequence but to those immediately interested, hung the destinies of a vast continent and the future balance of the universe. The events of our history are therefore not to be estimated by their apparent magnitude at the time they occurred. An obscure battle in the woods, between white men and Indians, often terminated the existence of a nation, and decided the mastery of territories now inhabited by increasing millions; and many are the forgotten acts of virtuous heroism which, in their consequences, outdo the victories of Alexander and Bonaparte. Their conquests are only recorded in history, and the world, which was rudely jostled out of place by their ambition, has returned again to its orbit. But the bow that was bent by the energies of the early settlers of our country has never become relaxed; nothing has gone back, every thing has moved, and is still moving, onward; and the actions I am now about to relate of Wash ington, though many of them in themselves of no great magnitude when clothed in words, if followed out in their consequences will be found to have carried with them effects that confer a degree of importance far, very far, beyond those of many of the most renowned warriors of ancient or modern times. If there ever was a people who should love and venerate their ancestors, it is the inhabitants of these United States, who have received from their sufferings and heroism the patrimony of a New World, the legacy of freedom and prosperity.

Washington having succeeded to that command, for which, it appears, he was originally intended, by the death of Colonel Fry, prepared for action with his usual decision and celerity. As the first military character in Virginia, though yet a mere youth, not quite twenty-one years old, he had been strongly spoken of for the command of this little force in the first in stance. But where others aspired to honours, he only laboured to deserve them. In a letter to a member of the House of Burgesses, he says, "The command of the whole force is what I neither look for, expect, or desire; for I am impartial enough to confess it is a charge too great for my youth and inexperience to be intrusted with. Knowing this, I have too sincere a love for my country to undertake that which may tend to her prejudice. But if I could entertain hopes that you thought me worthy of the post of Lieutenant-Colonel, and would favour me so far as to mention it at the appointment of officers, I could not but entertain a true sense of the kindness." Thus, on this, as on every other occasion of his life, did Washington exemplify the great truth that those who are most fitted for high stations are always the last to seek them.

At the head of only two companies of the regiment, to the command of which he soon succeeded, Washington, sometime in the spring of 1754, penetrated into the Alleghany mountains, to a place called the Great Meadows. The Blue Ridge was at that time the frontier of Virginia. The great valley between that and the Alleghanies, now one of the richest regions of the United States, was tenanted but by a few straggling settlers from Pennsylvania, whose voices were like one crying in the wilderness, and whose history is one of Indian wars and Indian massacre. Placed beyond the reach of the protection or of the restraint of the laws and institutions of the social state, they for several years maintained a sort of independent existence, governed by the statutes of necessity alone; making war against the wandering tribes of the neighbouring forests, either in self-defence or for purposes of vengeance, unchecked and unaided by the state government. The people thus situated, united only by the common tie of mutual dangers, although they partook of the habits and manners of social life, were as near a state of nature, as to government, as is compatible with civilization.

This position at the Great Meadows brought him in advance towards the French posts, and enabled Washington the better to protect the frontier of Virginia. While here, receiving information that the French had commenced hostilities by dispersing a party in the employment of the Ohio company, he advanced upon and surrounded a detachment, aided by a dark and rainy night. At the dawn of day, a fire was

commenced upon them, which killed their commander, upon which the rest immediately surrendered, with the exception of one man, who
escaped.

Reinforced by the arrival of the remainder
of the regiment, and by two companies of regular troops, Washington, after throwing up a
small intrenchment at the Great Meadows,
which he called Fort Necessity, and in the
erection of which he laboured with the rest, advanced on Fort Duquesne. This was now the
strong-hold of the French on the Ohio, and exhibited a testimony of the accuracy of his military judgment, having been erected on the very
spot indicated by Washington in his journal as
a fine military position. Early in his march,
however, he was met by a party of friendly Indians, who, in their figurative language, told
him the French and their copper-coloured con-
federates " were as numerous as the pigeons
in the woods, and coming like birds on the
wing."

By the advice of a council of war, it was now
determined to retreat to the Great Meadows.
Accordingly the little army returned to Fort
Necessity, where, before they could complete

their preparations for defence, they were attacked by De Villier at the head of fifteen hundred men, and forced to surrender, after a gallant defence. The garrison obtained the most honourable terms: they were allowed to march out with the honours of war, retaining their baggage and arms, and to return home without being molested.

Though the expedition proved unsuccessful, yet Washington in this, as in every other disaster of his life, acquired additional reputation. The legislature of Virginia gave a gratuity to the soldiers, and voted its thanks to the officers and their commander. Thus was this high honour conferred for the second time on a youth scarcely arrived at the age of manhood. A similar instance, I believe, does not occur in the history of this country. The gratuity to the privates, and the vote of thanks, were not unmerited, since it appears that the attack of the fort was sustained by not more than three hundred of the Virginia regiment, the remainder having retired on learning that the French and Indians were "as thick as pigeons in the woods."

Shortly after this event the military career

of Washington was arrested for a time by an ordinance of Governor Dinwiddie, regulating the rank of the provincial officers serving with those of his majesty's regular troops. These last were to take rank of all those commissioned by the colonial governors, without regard to date of commission. This was not all; insult and injustice was carried so far as to divest the general and field officers of the provincial troops of all rank when serving with those of a similar grade bearing the royal commission. The conduct of Washington may easily be anticipated. He disdained to acquiesce in this insulting preference, and declaring his willingness to serve his country at all times, when it did not carry with it the sacrifice of his honour, resigned his commission.

Being now, by the death of his brother Lawrence, which took place during his expedition to the Great Meadows, possessed of the estate of Mount Vernon, Washington retired thither to the enjoyment of those rural occupations and rural exercises which he loved next to the perils of war when encountered in the service of his country. But scarcely had he settled himself at this magnificent spot when the roar of can-

non was heard echoing along the Potomac, at
the opening of the spring of 1755. An English
squadron sailed up the river, landed an army
at Belhaven, now called Alexandria, under the
command of General Braddock, soon afterwards so famous for his obstinacy, imprudence,
and consequent disasters.

General Braddock had landed at the Capes
of Virginia, and proceeded to Williamsburg,
the seat of government, where he consulted
with Governor Dinwiddie. He inquired for
Colonel Washington, with whose character he
was well acquainted, and expressed a wish to
see him. On being informed of his resignation
and the cause, he is said to have exclaimed
that " he was a lad of sense and spirit, and had
acted as became a soldier and a man of hon
our." He immediately wrote him a pressing
invitation to assume the situation of volunteer
aid-de-camp, which involved no question of
rank, and which, after consultation with his
family, was accepted. Washington once more
resumed his military career by joining the
British forces at Belhaven.

These were shortly after reinforced by three
companies of Virginia riflemen, raised by an

act of the legislature, and consisting of as brave
hardy spirits as ever drew a trigger.   This accession made the army about two thousand
strong, and with these, in the month of June,
1755, Braddock set forth in his march through
the wilderness, from whence he and many
others of his companions never returned

CHAPTER IV.

Departure of Washington with Braddock's Army—Falls sick
and is left at the Great Meadows—Joins the Army the Day
before the Battle—His advice disregarded—The Army sur
prised and defeated—Braddock shot—Behaviour of Washington during the Fight—Retreat of the Army—Predictions
of the Old Indian Chief and the Rev. Mr. Davies—Sixteen
Companies raised, and the Command given to Washington—
Sufferings of the People of the Frontier from Indian Barbarity
—Difficulties in defending them—Picture of Washington in
his Uniform of Provincial Colonel—His Account of the Massacre of a Family by the Indians—Jealousy and Imbecility of
Governor Dinwiddie—Speech of Colonel Barrè—Lord Loudon—Franklin's Account of him—General Forbes—Expedition against, and Capture of, Fort Duquesne—War carried
to the Northern Frontier—Washington resigns his Com
mission.

THE troops under Braddock marched in two
divisions to the old station at the Little Meadows.   On the way, Washington was attacked
by a fever, and became so ill that the commanding officer insisted upon his remaining until the
rear of the army came up under Colonel Dunbar.   He consented, much against his will;

but the instant he was able, pushed on and joined Braddock the evening before he fell into that fatal ambuscade where he perished with many other gallant spirits, not in a blaze of glory, but in the obscurity of the dismal forests.

Washington, on rejoining the army, urged upon General Braddock the necessity of increasing and incessant caution. He dwelt much on the silent, unseen motions of the warriors of the woods, who come like birds on the wing, without being preceded by any indications of their approach, or leaving a trace behind them. But the fate of Braddock was decreed; or, rather, his own conduct sealed that destiny which ever follows at the heels of folly and imprudence. He despised the advice of wisdom and experience, and bitterly did he suffer the penalty. The silly pride of a British officer disdained the lessons of a provincial youth who had never fought on the bloody plains of Flanders. There can be no doubt that the superiority affected by the natives of England over those of the American colonies, was one of the silent yet effective causes of the Revolution.

The army halted at Cumberland for some days and then proceeded to its ruin. Contrary to the advice of Washington, who wished to lead with his Virginians, the British grenadiers marched in front about half a mile ahead; the Virginia troops followed; and the rest of the army brought up the rear. The ground was covered with whortleberry bushes reaching to the horses' bellies until they gained the top of a hill, which commanded an extensive prospect far ahead. Here a council was held, during which, the traditionary authority I follow describes Braddock as standing with a fusee in his right hand, the breech on the ground, and rubbing the leaves with his toe as if in great perplexity, without saying a word.

The consultation over, they proceeded onward through the deep woods, the order of march being changed, and the infantry in advance. When within about seven miles of Fort Duquesne, and passing through a narrow defile, a fire from some ambushed enemy arrested their march and laid many a soldier dead on the ground. Nothing was seen but the smoke of the unerring rifle rising above the tops of the woods, and nothing heard but the report of the fatal weapons. There was a dead silence among the savages and their allies, who, masked behind the trees, were equally invisible with the great king of terrors whose work they were performing.

The army of Braddock and the general himself were both taken by surprise, and the consequence was a total neglect or forgetfulness of the proper mode of defence or attack. After a few discharges from the unseen destroyers in the wood, Washington remained of all the aids alive. In fact, the whole duties of the day devolved on him, and the entire resistance on the troops of Virginia. He exposed himself to thousands of unerring marksmen; his clothes were perforated with bullets, and twice was his horse shot under him. Yet he escaped without a wound, as if to justify the prediction of the old Indian warrior that led the hostile savages, who used long afterwards to declare— "That man was never to be killed by a bullet, for he had seventeen times had a fair shot at him with his rifle, yet could not bring him down."

All accounts agree that the unfortunate Braddock behaved with great gallantry, though with little discretion, in this trying situation. He encouraged his soldiers, and was crying out with his speaking-trumpet, " Hurrah, boys ! ose the saddle or win the horse !" when a bullet struck him, and he fell to the ground, exclaiming—"Ha, boys ! I'm gone !" During all this time not a cannon had been fired by the British forces. It was at this moment that one who was with him at the time, who is still living, and on whose humble testimony I rely even with more confidence than on the more imposing authority of history, thus describes Washington. " I saw him take hold of a brass field-piece, as if it had been a stick. He looked like a fury ; he tore the sheet lead from the touch-hole ; he placed one hand on the muzzle, the other on the breech ; he pulled with this, and pushed with that, and wheeled it round as if it had been nothing. It tore the ground like a barshare.* The powder-monkey rushed up with the fire, and then the cannon began to bark, I tell you. They fought and they fought, and the Indians began to *holla*, when the rest of the brass cannon made the bark of the trees fly, and the Indians come down. That place they

* A kind of plough.

call Rock Hill, and there they left five hundred men dead on the ground."

The army of Braddock suffered a total defeat. The survivors retreated across the Monongahela, where they rested, and the general breathed his last. His gallant behaviour during the trying situation in which he was placed, and his death, which in some measure paid the penalty of his foolhardihood, have preserved to his memory some little respect, and for his fate perhaps more sympathy than it merited. He was one of those military men of little character and desperate fortune which mother countries are accustomed to send out for the purpose of foraging in the rich fields of their colonies. He was succeeded in his command by Colonel Dunbar, who ordered all the stores, except such as were indispensably necessary, to be destroyed, and sought safety, with the remainder of his European troops, in the distant repose of the city of Philadelphia, where he placed the army in winter-quarters in the dog days, leaving Virginia to the protection of her gallant rangers.

The conduct of the British troops on this occasion was, though perhaps natural in the terrible and untried situation in which they were placed, such as to excite the contempt of Washington and his provincials, to whom the escape of the surviving regulars was entirely owing. It was he and they that exclusively made head against the invisible enemy, and finally so checked his proceedings as to secure a quiet retreat to a place of security. But for them, in all probability, scarce a man would have escaped. The British officers behaved with great gallantry, and upwards of sixty of them were either killed or wounded; but the privates exhibited nothing but cowardice, confusion, and disobedience; and it seems quite probable that Washington here learned a secret which was of infinite service in his future career by teaching him that British grenadiers were not invincible.

The provincial troops, on the contrary, according to the testimony of Washington, "behaved like men," to use his own language. Out of three companies that were in the action but thirty survived. The regulars, on the contrary, "ran away like sheep before hounds," leaving every thing to the mercy of the enemy. "When we endeavoured to rally them," continues Washington, in his letter to the governor of Virginia, " in hopes of regaining the ground we had lost, and what was left on it, it was with as little success as if we had attempted to have stopped the wild bears of the mountains, or the rivulets with our feet."

The conduct of Washington on this trying occasion confirmed him in the affections and confidence of Virginia, and gave occasion to more than one presage of his future eminence. Among the rest, the Rev. Mr. Davies, in a sermon preached soon after Braddock's defeat, taking occasion to allude to an event which was fraught with such disastrous consequences, uttered the following sentence, which long afterwards was considered prophetic—" I cannot but hope," he said, " that Providence has preserved this youth to be the saviour of his country."

But such predictions rest on the experience of the past, not on an insight into the future. The inspiration which dictated the sentiment of Mr. Davies, was, without doubt, founded on the solid basis of an accurate knowledge of the virtues, acquirements, and character of Washington. These furnished the best auguries of the future, and bore a sure testimony that, should the period ever arrive when their exercise would become necessary to the salvation of his country, she would be saved by Washington.

The Virginia Assembly being in session when the news of Braddock's defeat and death, and Dunbar's ignominious desertion, arrived, at once saw the dangers to which the province was now exposed. Sixteen companies were accordingly raised, the command of which was offered to Washington, accompanied by the rare compliment of permission to name his field officers. This offer was cheerfully accepted, though it necessarily imposed on him a charge of the most critical nature. The whole frontier of Virginia, extending three hundred and sixty miles, now lay exposed to the incursions of hordes of savages, whose amusement was midnight murders; whose fury spared neither age nor sex; whose enmity was insatiable; whose revenge, inexpressibly terrible. The means possessed by the province were inadequate to the purposes of effectual protection; the British government had deserted them, or at least was ignorant of the desertion of Dunbar; the royal governor was inefficient, jealous, or indifferent,

and the safety of Virginia depended on herself
alone. Her arms were courage and patriot
ism—her tutelary genius was Washington.

The savages had already commenced their
bloody career, accompanied, and, if not instigated, at least not controlled by their allies;
and now was seen what has so often disgraced
the Christian name in this New World, the association of those whose religion is mercy and
forgiveness, with those who never forgive. A
scene ensued which, if I could prevail upon
myself to enter on its terrible details, would
thrill the hearts of my young readers, and make
them shiver as with an ague. Civilized warfare, in its worst aspect, is nothing compared
with the strife of the wilderness with wild and
savage warriors, painted like fiends, and yelling
like infuriated madmen. This for ages was
the destiny of your forefathers, my young
readers, and never should you forget the sacred
duty of affectionate gratitude to their memory.
They won for you a dearbought prize, and left
you a noble legacy, which you will one day
learn to cherish as inestimable.

Now came the time that tried men's souls
and bodies too. The pagan redmen and their

Christian allies scoured the whole frontier of Virginia, and the wretched inhabitants, scattered at far distances from each other, in scanty numbers that precluded effectual resistance suffered all the horrors of savage cruelty, instigated and abetted by the arts of civilized white men. Nothing was spared; no age, no sex, no man, woman, or child, could hope for mercy, living or dead; for the revenge of the red man is not satiated by murder; it outlives the death of its victim, and wreaks its last efforts on the inanimate body. The smoke of burning cottages, and the shrieks of murdered victims, were seen and heard to arise from the depths of the forests, and the repose of nature was disturbed by Indian yells and dying groans mingled in one horrible concert. Fifteen hundred savages, divided into separate parties, scoured the frontier, and, penetrating towards the more compact settlements, carried terror and ruin in their train. All who did not flee were murdered and scalped, and in a few months the frontier was a desert and a grave.

In this cruel state of things, the hopes of Virginia rested on Washington and her own means of defence Dunbar was at Philadel.

phia; the governor was suspected of being
jealous of the reputation of the rising hero, and
of that acquired by the provincial troops, whose
conduct at the fatal defeat of Braddock was
contrasted with that of the boasted and boasting regulars; and the province was left to her
own limited resources. Fort Duquesne, the
great head-quarters of the empire of the forest,
was in the hands of the French; the Indian
tribes of the West were, without exception, under their influence, and a frontier of three hundred and sixty miles was to be defended by
seven hundred militia. But these were commanded by Washington.

He was but twenty-two years of age when
he accepted the arduous task of defending his
country from Christian ambition, savage fury,
and remorseless revenge. Nothing but the purest
motives of patriotism could have prompted him
to undertake such a duty with the means at his
command. The force raised for this purpose
was utterly inadequate to protect the extensive
line now exposed to the incursions of the savages and their instigators. To keep it together
would be to leave a great portion of the State
unprotected; to divide it into small parties

would be to ensure their destruction. Scanty as this force was, it was deficient in supplies of every kind. If he fought the enemy in mass, he would certainly be beaten; if he declined, he would as certainly be blamed. Every savage murder would recoil on his head, and every burning cottage light up a flame of indignation against him. Add to this, that the old royal governor was now ill-disposed towards him, not only on the score of his popularity, but his firm and manly remonstrances whenever he felt himself called upon to point out the existence of errors or neglect, and the means of remedying or avoiding them in future.

It was in the midst of such difficulties, embarrassments, and mortifications, that Washington became schooled to that patience, fortitude, and perseverance, which prepared him to encounter the obstacles that everywhere presented themselves at the commencement and through the whole progress of that great Revolution which he consummated by his talents and his patriotism. The royal governor, with the usual wisdom of such dignitaries as generally fall to the lot of colonies, had determined to act on the defensive There was no hope

of being able to conquer Fort Duquesne, the
possession of which enabled the French to
command the Ohio and influence the Indians.
Washington therefore proceeded to establish, as
far as practicable with his limited means, a
chain of small forts along the frontier, in which
he placed the principal part of his little army.
With the remainder he traversed the frontier
for the purpose of arresting and punishing the
depredations of the savages, and this service he
performed with a vigour and celerity that will
never be forgotten by Virginia.

In the course of three years of incessant toil,
exposure, privations, and dangers, he was wit-
ness to a succession of scenes, the particular
relation of which would swell this volume beyond its salutary limits, and at the same time
serve to exemplify the barbarities of savage
warfare, as well as the unconquerable firmness and vigour of this admirable young man.
At an age when too many of our youth are either
engaged in frivolous amusements, or murdering
their precious time in the indulgence of degrading passions that equally destroy the body
and corrupt the mind, Washington was occu
pied night and day in the highest duties of a

patriot, defending the unprotected, shielding the
bare bosom of his country, and laying the foundation of a fame as lasting as it is pure and un-
defiled.   It is sufficient for my purpose to say,
that all that imagination ever conceived, or experience realized of cruelty, suffering, and despair,
was presented in the three years of savage warfare which succeeded the defeat of Braddock.

Traversing the wilderness where here and
there a log-house, or a little cluster of log-
houses, with a cultivated spot around them, had
a few days before, perhaps, presented a smiling
picture of the first efforts of man to cope with
the wild luxuriance of nature, he would come
to a pile of smoking ruins, over which the birds
of prey were soaring, and around which the
hungry wolves were yelping and howling.
Their prey was the mangled, perhaps half-con-
sumed, body of a helpless woman, an innocent
girl, or a speechless infant that never drew
nourishment but from the breast of its mother.
Mangled with the knife or the tomahawk,
or perforated with bullet-holes—their bodies
scorched black with fire, and half devoured by
beasts and birds of prey—their head stripped
of its covering of hair by the crooked scalping-

knife, they lay festering in the sun, sad monuments of savage revenge, or bloody ferocity.

The history of no people that ever existed affords such a succession of dangers, hardships, and sufferings as were encountered by the ancestors of my young readers. They came from the enjoyment and habits of civilized life to the untracked wilderness, or, what is still worse, a wilderness tracked only by a race of wild redmen, the most impracticable in their barbarism, the most unforgiving in their hate, of any recorded in the annals of the world. They endured all, suffered all, conquered all and though they had sowed their seed in dangers and terrors besetting them on every side, it did not fall on rocks and barren places. It grew and flourished, and extended into a rich and glorious harvest, which those who are now reaping should repay by venerating their virtues and imitating their example.

Washington was not accustomed to dwell on this, one of the most painful and arduous periods of his life. But there is one tale of horror which he related on a particular occasion when questioned on the subject by a cherished friend, which will give some idea of scenes that were of almost daily occurrence during these gloomy and disastrous times. It has been preserved, as nearly as possible, in his own words, by one whose situation afforded him the best means of information.

"One day," said Washington, " as we were traversing a part of the frontier, we came upon a single log-house, standing in the centre of a little clearing surrounded by woods on all sides As we approached we heard the report of a gun, the usual signal of coming horrors. Our party crept cautiously through the underwood, until we approached near enough to see what we had already foreboded. A smoke was slowly making its way through the roof of the house, while at the same moment a party of Indians came forth laden with plunder, consisting of clothes, domestic utensils, household furniture, and dripping scalps. We fired, and killed all but one, who tried to get away, but was soon shot down.

"On entering the hut we saw a sight that, though we were familiar with blood and massacre, struck us, at least myself, with feelings more mournful than I had ever experienced before. On a bed in one corner of the room lay the body of a young woman swimming in blood,

with a gash in her forehead which almost sepa
rated the head into two parts. On her breast lay
two little babes, apparently twins, less than a
twelvemonth old, with their heads also cut
open.   Their innocent blood, which had once
flowed in the same veins, now mingled in one
current again.   I was inured to scenes of
bloodshed and misery, but this cut me to the
soul, and never in my after-life did I raise my
hand against a savage without calling to mind
the mother with her little twins, their heads
cleft asunder.

" On examining the tracks of the Indians to
see what other murders they might have committed, we found a little boy, and a few steps
beyond his father, both scalped, and both stone
dead.   From the prints of the feet of the boy,
it would seem he had been following the plough
with his father, who being probably shot down,
he had attempted to escape.   But the poor boy
was followed, overtaken, and murdered.   The
ruin was complete.   Not one of the family had
been spared. ˙Such was the character of our
miserable warfare.   The wretched people on
the frontier never went to rest without bidding
each other farewell; for the chances were they

might never wake again, or awake only to find their last sleep. On leaving one spot for the purpose of giving protection to another point of exposure, the scene was often such as I shall never forget. The women and children clung round our knees, beseeching us to stay and protect them, and crying out for God's sake not to leave them to be butchered by the savages. A hundred times, I declare to Heaven, I would have laid down my life with pleasure, even under the tomahawk and scalping-knife, could I have ensured the safety of those suffering people by the sacrifice."

The difficulties of his situation were aggravated by malicious reports and insinuations, reflecting on his conduct and capacity in those miserable times. He was assailed by secret enemies, who poisoned the mind of Governor Dinwiddie, and added to his unwillingness to give efficient aid to the conduct of this distressing war. There are extant letters of Washington to that officer, vindicating his proceedings with a manly firmness, joined to a modesty highly becoming, and calling for the names of his secret accusers. In the midst of these insidious attacks he however always had one great consolation in the consciousness of performing his arduous duties to the extent of his power, and the increasing confidence of his countrymen. Those sufferings which he could not prevent by his valour, he predicted by his sagacity, and every failure of measures which he had endeavoured to prevent only served to prove his superiority over those whose orders he was obliged to obey. Thus he rose with the calamities of the times, and shone only the brighter for the darkness which surrounded him.

To make matters still worse, and increase the miseries of Virginia, the British ministry sent out Lord Loudon, as governor and commander-in-chief. Franklin has given his character, and pronounces it entirely made up of "indecision." "He was like St. George on the signs, always on horseback, but never rode on." It may be supposed, that under such a commander-in-chief matters could only become worse than they were before. Washington presented him with a statement, in which, with his usual directness and brevity, he pointed out the fatal consequences of that system of defensive operations he had been compelled to adopt, de-

tailed the destitute situation of his troops, and
urged an immediate attack on Fort Duquesne,
the possession of which by the British could,
he foresaw, alone secure the people of Virginia
from the calamities they were now suffering.

But the views of Lord Loudon were directed
to another quarter. He aspired to the con
quest of Canada. His plan was to invade that
province with the great body of his forces,
leaving only twelve hundred men to guard the
whole southern frontier. Virginia was thus
not only left to protect herself, but to assist in
the defence of the weaker colonies of the South.
But the maxim and the practice of Washington
was never to abandon his exertions in a good
cause. He turned upon Lieutenant-Governor
Dinwiddie and to the assembly of Virginia, once
more urging the importance of a proper organization of the militia and the raising of a regular
force. But it was his fate in almost every period of his life to feel and to suffer from the
consequences of legislative folly or inactivity.
His remonstrances were not only disregarded,
but the effective force was diminished instead
of being increased. Almost any other man
would have retired from such a service in dis

gust; but Washington, happily for his country, was one of those to whom the neglect and inefficiency of others were only stimulatives to new exertions and new sacrifices.

He urged and reurged the capture of Fort Duquesne, which he had learned was only garrisoned by three hundred men. But that system of defensive warfare, which he from the first strenuously opposed, and which fatal experience had proved to be altogether nugatory, was still continued, and produced only a repetition of calamities. A second time the savages and their allies broke in upon the frontier, approaching still nearer to the older settlements, laying waste the country west of the Blue Ridge, and spreading destruction to life and property wherever they came. Another succession of unheard-of barbarities desolated the land, and the boasted protection of the mother country was exemplified in the triumphs of the tomahawk and scalping-knife, the murder of defenceless women and children. Well might Colonel Barrè exclaim, in a burst of spontaneous eloquence which has scarcely ever been equalled, when one of the ministers in a debate in the Brititish Parliament asked,

" Are not the Americans our children ; planted by our care, nourished by our indulgence, and protected by our arms ?" Well might he exclaim :—

" *They* planted by your care ! No, sir ; your oppressions planted them in America. They fled from your tyranny to an uncultivated and inhospitable land, where they were exposed to all the evils and sufferings which a wilderness alive with bloodthirsty savages could inflict. Yet, inspired by a true English love of liberty, they thought nothing of these, compared with those they had suffered in their own country, and from you who ought to have been their protectors.

" *They* nourished by your indulgence ! No, sir ; they grew by your neglect. Your indulgence consisted in sending them hungry packs of your own creatures to spy out their liberties, that you might assail them by encroachments ; to misrepresent their actions, and to prey upon their substance. Yes, sir ; you sent them men whose conduct has often caused the blood of these children of freedom to boil in their veins ; men, promoted to the highest seats of justice in that country, who, to my knowledge, had good reason to dread a court of justice at home.

"*They* protected by your arms! No, sir; they have nobly taken up arms in your cause, not their own. They are fighting the battles of your ambition, not their interests; they have exerted a most heroic valour in the midst of their daily labours, for the defence of a country whose frontier was drenched in blood, while its interior contributed all its savings for your emolument."

Soon after the arrival of Lord Loudon, Governor Dinwiddie departed from Virginia, leaving behind him but an indifferent reputation and a wretched province exposed to all the horrors of Indian warfare. The administration of the government devolved, for a short time, on Mr. Blair, who, during his brief authority, cordially co-operated with Washington in all his measures for the public security. Lord Loudon, after doing nothing, returned to England, and General Abercrombie succeeded him as commander-in-chief of all the British forces in the colonies. The war in the south was committed to the charge of General Forbes, who, influenced by the strong solicitations of Wasnington, at length determined on an attack upon Fort Duquesne. Before, however, his preparations were completed, the savages and their allies a third time poured in on the few remaining inhabitants of the frontier, and completed the sad history of these disastrous times by new conflagrations and massacres. Having done this, they departed to their wilderness again, unmolested, and laden with plunder and bloody trophies.

At length, in the year 1758, General Forbes put his army in motion for the purpose of dislodging the French from their strong-hold at the confluence of the Alleghany and Monongahela. I have now before me the plan of a line of march proposed by Washington and adopted by the commanding general. It displays a perfect knowledge of the peculiarities of Indian warfare, and of the means by which they are best counteracted. Though distinguished by that rare modesty which was the characteristic of Washington in every circumstance and situation of life, there is in the language and sentiments a manly firmness, indicating not only a conviction of right, but a con sciousness of superiority. His long experience in this species of warfare had given him a privilege to advise.

But though the royal general accepted the plan, he did not follow the advice by which it was accompanied. Washington knew the importance, nay, the absolute necessity, of celerity. Arrangements had been made for forming a junction with the warriors of some Indian tribes which were inclined to desert the French cause, and they were now waiting at Winchester for that purpose. He predicted, knowing the impatient disposition of these wild warriors of the woods, that they would become tired and go home; and so it happened. The season was half over before the army arrived at Winchester, previous to which, the savages had left that place, and crossed the Alleghanies.

It was the latter end of June before General Forbes left Winchester, and Washington again had occasion to predict the failure of these dilatory operations. As if studious of delays, the commander, instead of marching by Braddock's road, as it was called, where a passage was already opened through the wilderness, determined to cut a new path from a place called

Raystown, against the opinions and remonstrances of Washington. He foresaw the consequences of such a tedious operation, and anticipated the failure of the expedition. In one of his letters, he says, " If General Forbes persists at this late season, he will certainly ruin the attempt."

On another occasion, alluding to these pernicious delays, he says, " If this conduct of our leaders does not originate in superior orders, it must proceed from weakness too gross to name. Nothing but a miracle can bring this campaign to a happy issue." He predicted that the army would be obliged to winter at Laurel Hill, without gathering any laurels, and that Fort Duquesne would not be captured till the next year, if it was ever captured. After cutting this new road through the wilderness, a work of vast labour and consequent delay, they reached Laurel Hill some time in the middle of November, and a council of war was called to decide upon the propriety of going into winter-quarters here, or turning back upon Winchester.

While actually thus employed, some prisoners, who had been accidentally captured, disclosed the almost defenceless state of Fort Du quesne. The design of the British government to attack Canada having become known to the French governor, he had withdrawn all the force from the Ohio for his defence at home, with the exception of about three hundred men. The Indians, who always join what they consider the strongest side in their co-operation with white men, deserted their French allies, and the British commander was assured that the fort was incapable of defence, and would surrender without firing a gun. Encouraged by the news, he changed his plan. Instead of wintering at Laurel Hill or returning to Winchester, he marched upon Fort Duquesne, which was evacuated by the garrison on his approach. After setting fire to the buildings, they embarked in their boats, sailed down the Ohio, and the French power ceased for ever in that part of the world.

Thenceforward, until the capture of Quebec by General Wolfe, and the final extinction of the French empire in North America, the tide of war flowed in a direction towards the north. The plains of Abraham, the pass of Ticonderoga, the Lakes Champlain and George, and the frontier of New-York became the aceldama the field of blood in the New World.   Virginia ceased to bleed for a time; her harrassed citizens slept quietly in their beds; her gallant rangers reposed from their toils; and the Indian warwhoop was heard no more.

Having nobly performed his duty to his country in her hour of peril, and seen those objects gained which he had sought through years of danger, suffering, and disappointment, Washington now resigned his commission, and sought repose in the shades of Mount Vernon. His arduous exertions and severe exposures in the service of his beloved countrymen had impaired in a considerable degree his naturally fine constitution, while his incessant public duties necessarily prevented a proper attention to his domestic affairs.   These considerations determined his conduct, and at the close of the year 1758, he bade adieu to his brothers in arms, who answered him by an affectionate address, and retired to the bosom of tranquillity, there to remain till called forth to the fulfilment of a destiny, as high as ever fell to the lot of man.

He was now only twenty-seven years of age, and yet had twice received the thanks of the representatives of the people of Virginia.   His character was firmly established for integrity, firmness, patriotism, and military skill. Everywhere he was looked up to as the first of the sons of Virginia; as her sword and shield; as one who in the hour of danger or difficulty might be safely relied on as a sage in council, a hero in battle. He had already earned the most precious of all sublunary rewards, the confidence and affections of his countrymen. Such are the fruits of early exertion in a virtuous cause, and such the blessings of a well-spent youth

CHAPTER V.

Marriage—Domestic Life and Habits of Washington—First
Meeting with Mrs. Custis—Picture of that Lady at the Time
she captivated Washington—Old Jeremy—His Conversations
—Sketch of Mount Vernon—Division of Washington's Time
—Hours of rising, retiring to rest, breakfasting, dining, &c.—
His Temperance—Kindness to his Relatives residing at
Mount Vernon—Discipline of his Servants—Extracts from
his old Almanac of 1762—His Custom of retiring to read—
Anecdote of Old Jeremy—Troubles with England—Is elected
to the First Congress.

I AM now to present Washington to the contemplation of my young readers in a character
not less worthy of their admiration, and in
which they may all imitate him if they please.
The ensuing fifteen years of his life were spent
in rural occupations, rural exercises, and the
performance of his duties as a husband, a master, and a farmer, occasionally interrupted by
those of a justice of the peace and a member of the Virginia Assembly. In the latter
capacity he was a highly useful legislator, but

too much a man of energy and action to be a
great orator, although admirably clear in his in-
tellect, and dignified in deportment.   I have indeed observed that few of the celebrated orators
of ancient or modern times were ever much
distinguished for military skill and prowess.
Many who can tell how a thing should be done,
are utterly incapable of doing it, and it has
passed into a proverb, that those who are good
at talking are seldom good at any thing else.

Soon after his retirement from the service,
he married Mrs. Martha Custis, a lady born
in the same year with himself, of considerable
personal attractions, and large fortune.   Her
maiden name was Dandridge, and both by birth
and marriage she was connected with some of
the most respectable families in Virginia.   All her
claims to distinction from family connections are
now, however, merged in the one great name of
Washington, and derive their purest lustre from
an association with the Father of his Country.

It has been related to me by one whose authority I cannot doubt, that the first meeting of
Colonel Washington with his future wife was
entirely accidental, and took place at the house
of Mr. Chamberlayne, who resided on the Pa-

munkey, one of the branches of York River. Washington was on his way to Williamsburg, on somewhat pressing business, when he met Mr. Chamberlayne, who, according to the good old Virginia custom, which forbids a traveller to pass the door without doing homage at the fireside of hospitality, insisted on his stopping an hour or two at his mansion. Washington complied unwillingly, for his business was urgent. But it is said that he was in no haste to depart, for he had met the lady of his fate in the person of Mrs. Martha Custis, of the White House, county of New Kent, in Virginia.

I have now before me a copy of an original picture of this lady, taken about the time of which I am treating, when she captivated the affections of Washington. It represents a figure rather below the middle size, with hazel eyes, and hair of the same colour, finely rounded arms, a beautiful chest and taper waist, dressed in a blue silk robe of the fashion of the times, and altogether furnishing a very sufficient apology to a young gentleman of seven and twenty for delaying his journey, and perhaps forgetting his errand for a time. The sun went down and rose again before Washington departed for Williamsburg, leaving his heart behind him, and, perhaps, carrying another away in exchange. Having completed his business at the seat of government, he soon after visited the White House, and being accustomed, as my informant says, to energetic and persevering action, won the lady and carried her off from a crowd of rivals.

The marriage took place in the winter of 1759, but at what precise date is not to be found in any record, nor is it, I believe, within the recollection of any person living. I have in my possession a manuscript containing the particulars of various conversations with old Jeremy, Washington's black servant, who was with him at Braddock's defeat, and accompanied him on his wedding expedition to the White House. Old Jeremy is still living, while I am now writing, and in full possession of his faculties. His memory is most especially preserved, and, as might be expected, he delights to talk of Massa George. The whole series of conversations was taken down verbatim, in the peculiar phraseology of the old man, and it is quite impossible to read the record of this living chronicle of the early days of Washington, without receiving the full conviction of its perfect truth.

From this period Washington resided constantly at Mount Vernon, one of the most beautiful situations in the world. A wood-crowned bluff of considerable height projects out into the Potomac, here one of the most capacious and noble of rivers, affording an extensive view both above and below. A fine lawn slopes gracefully from the piazza in front of the house to the brow of the hill, where, high above the wave, you stand and view a wide prospect of great variety and interest. The house was at the time of his marriage of indifferent size and convenience, but was shortly improved into a capacious and imposing mansion. The place is worthy of him with whose memory it is inseparably associated, and long may it appertain to the family and name of Washington.

He here put in practice that system of regularity and of temperance in every species of indulgence and of labour, which he persevered in, as far as was consistent with his circumstances and situation, during the remainder of his life. His moments were numbered, and divided, and devoted to his various objects and pursuits. His hours of rising and going to bed were the same throughout every season of the year. He always shaved, dressed himself, and answered his letters by candle-light in summer and winter; and his time for retiring to rest was nine o'clock, whether he had company or not. He breakfasted at seven o'clock in summer, and eight in winter; dined at two, and drank his tea, of which he was very fond, early in the evening, never taking any supper. His breakfast always consisted of four small corn-cakes, split, buttered, and divided into quarters, with two small-sized cups of tea. At dinner he ate with a good appetite, but was not choice of his food; drank small-beer at his meals, and two glasses of old Madeira after the cloth was removed. He scarcely ever exceeded that quantity. The kernels of two or three black-walnuts completed the repast. He was very kind, affectionate, and attentive to his family, scrupulously observant of every thing relating to the comfort, as well as the deportment and manners, of the younger members.

His habits of military command produced a similar system with regard to his servants, of whom he exacted prompt attention and obedi ence. These conditions complied with, and they were sure of never being subjected to caprice or passion. Neglect or ill-conduct was promptly noticed, for the eye of the master was everywhere, and nothing connected with the economy of his estate escaped him. He knew the value of independence, and the mode by which it is obtained and preserved. With him idleness was an object of contempt, and prodigality of aversion. He never murdered an hour in wilful indolence, or wasted a dollar in worthless enjoyment. He was as free from extravagance as from meanness or parsimony, and never in the whole course of his life did he turn his back on a friend, or trifle with a creditor.

In an old Virginia almanac of 1762, belonging to Washington, and now before me, interleaved with blank sheets, are various memoranda relating to rural affairs, all in his own handwriting, a few of which I shall extract, for the purpose of showing my youthful readers that an attention to his private affairs was not considered beneath the dignity of the man destined o wield the fortunes of his country.

> *April* 5. Sowed timothy-seed in the old ap-
> ple-orchard below the hill.
> " 7. Sowed, or rather sprinkled a little
> of ditto on the oats.
> " 26. Began to plant corn at all my plan-
> tations.
> *May* 4. Finished planting corn at all my
> plantations.

Thus, in the dignified simplicity of usefulness did this great and good man employ himself during the years which elapsed between the period of his retirement after the expulsion of the French from the Ohio, until the commencement of the troubles which preceded the Revolution. His occupation was husbandry—the noblest of all others; his principal amusement was hunting the deer, which at that time abounded in the forests of the Potomac. Here his skill in horsemanship rendered him conspicuous above all his competitors. He also read much, and his hour was early in the morning.

His custom was to retire to a private room, where no one was permitted to interrupt him. Much curiosity prevailed among the servants to know what he was about, and old Jeremy relates that, in order to gratify it, he one morning entered the room under pretence of bringing a pair of boots. Washington, who was reading, raised his eyes from the book, and getting quietly up,—"I tell you," said Jeremy, "I go out of de room faster dan I come in!"

During this long interruption of his military life, Washington was, either constantly or at short intervals, a member of the Virginia Assembly, where he resolutely and firmly opposed the claims of British supremacy that now became daily more importunate and tenacious. The British officers serving under Braddock, Loudon, Forbes, and others, having been frequently entertained in the houses of the planters of Virginia, with all the appurtenances of apparent wealth, had carried home to England reports of the luxuries enjoyed and dispensed by these prosperous colonists. The general opinion in that State has always been, that these disclosures of unsuspected wealth first gave the British ministry an idea of taxing the colonies. There is also a tradition that a certain wealthy Virginian, being on a visit to England, engaged in play with the old Duke of Cumberland, the victor of Culloden, and lost, I think, twenty thousand pounds, which he paid promptly by a check on his banker. This fact becoming known, the ministry naturally concluded, that colonies affording such pigeons as this, might reasonably be called upon to pay for what they were pleased to call the protection of the mother country. The source from which this anecdote is derived entitles it to entire credit.

But whatever may have been the immediate causes, the time was now approaching when the repose of Washington, and the liberties of his fellow-citizens, were to be assailed by the pretensions of power. The claim of the mother country was to a right to tax the colonies through the agency of a parliament in which they were not represented; the great principle asserted by the colonies was, that taxation and representation were inseparable; in other words, that no subjects could, under the constitution of England, be taxed except by their own consent, through their own representatives, elected by themselves. The one stood upon its prerogative, the other on its rights enjoyed in common with all Englishmen. Perseverance on one hand, produced resistance on the other; and, as if *nations* could ever become rebels, the virtuous opposition of a whole people was stigmatized by the advocates of parliamentary supremacy as rebellion. At that period, colonies were considered to have no rights but such as were conceded to them at the pleasure of the mother country, and might be reclaimed under almost any pretence whatever. More degraded than even conquered provinces, they were treated neither as friends or foes; their industry was made tributary to the government at home, under pretence of paying for its protection, which protection was but another name for oppression; and their inhabitants insulted by arrogant assumptions of affected superiority, on the part of those who fattened on their spoils. Though the uniform practice of all modern governments had sanctioned these exercises of maternal despotism, it was still an unnatural state of things, and the only cement of such an unequal union was power on one hand, weakness on the other. It might have been foreseen, for all the attributes of our nature point to such a result, that the descendants of Englishmen, who, a great portion of them, had sacrificed their birthright and their home to escape oppression, would submit to it abroad not a moment after they could hope to resist it with success. Accordingly the assertion of the claim to tax the United Colonies of North America, was the signal for a successful resistance, the example of which has extended, or will extend, through the whole of this great continent—perhaps through the whole world—and which has established the temple of liberty on a basis which it is humbly hoped may never be overthrown.

The principles of freedom which had been implanted in this country with the first seed that was sown, now strengthened and expanded under threats and coercion; the storm that at first threatened from afar off, like a mere point in the horizon, now gathered, spread, and blackened into deeper hues, and the high-hearted, deep-reaching patriots of the west at once saw the certainty of war or submission.

"We must fight, Mr. Speaker—I repeat —we must fight!" was the prediction of Patrick Henry, and all reflecting persons recognised its truth. A Congress met at Philadelphia to concentrate and express the force and feelings of the colonies; Washington was elected a member, and breaking away at the call of his country from the happiness of rural life, and the delights of domestic associations, once more embarked on the waves that were finally to bear his country to the haven of a safe and honourable independence—himself to the highest pinnacle of glory.

CHAPTER VI.

Washington called from his Retirement to attend the first
Congress at Philadelphia—His Age and Appearance—His
Strength and Activity—Anecdote of Mr. Peale—Portrait
painted by him—Anecdote related by a Servant of Washington—Particular Description of his person—Is chosen Commander-in-chief—His Letters to Mrs. Washington, on accepting and departing to assume the Command—The Consequences to which he exposed himself in so doing—State of
the Public Mind—Ideas of Europe, and especially English
Superiority—Arrival and Reception at Boston—Situation of
the Army.

AT the period when Washington was called
from his dignified and happy repose at Mount
Vernon he was about forty-three years old, the
very prime of manhood. Exercise, temperance, wholesome employment, and a well-regu-
lated mind, had all combined to re-establish his
health, which had been somewhat impaired by
hard service in the wilderness, and to restore tha
vigour and activity for which in his youth he

had been so highly distinguished. It may not
be uninteresting to my young readers to describe
him as he is represented in a portrait painted at
Mount Vernon in 1772 by the elder Mr. Peale,
a copy of which is now before me. That worthy old gentleman used often in his latter days
to relate that, while engaged in this work, he
was one day amusing himself with the young
men of the family in playing at quoits and other
exercises, when Washington joined, and completely outdid them all.

As nothing relating to the Father of his Country can be uninteresting to his children, I will
here give another little anecdote illustrating his
strength, in the words of one of his nearest
connections, who is still living.

"We were sitting," said he, "in the little par-
lour fronting the river, to the right as you enter
the portico. The general and several others
were present—among them two young men remarkable for their strength, when a large back-
log rolled from the chimney out on the hearth.
The general took the tongs and very delibe-
rately, without apparent effort, put it back in
its place. A quarter of an hour afterwards he
went out, and the ease with which he handled

it became the subject of remark. The log was taken down, and not a man of us could lift, much less put it in place again. Finally, one with the tongs, another with the shovel, we all set to, and succeeded in replacing it. The general, though remarkably strong in all his limbs, was particularly so in his hands and fingers."

The portrait to which I refer, and which was taken shortly before Washington entered on his last and great career, represents a man in the vigour of his prime, in the uniform of the provincial troops; a cocked hat of the fashion of the times; a blue coat, faced and lined with scarlet; waistcoat and breeches of the same colour. The coat and waistcoat, in the left-hand pocket of which is seen a paper endorsed " Order of march," are both edged with silver lace, and the buttons of white metal. A gorget, shaped like a crescent, and bearing the arms of England, is suspended from the neck by a blue riband, and an embroidered lilac-coloured crape sash thrown over the left shoulder. The right hand is partly thrust into the waistcoat, and covered with a thick buff buckskin glove, and the left arm is passed behind the back so as to sustain a fusee, the barrel of which projects above the shoulder. This was the very dress he wore on the fatal field of Rock Hill, where Braddock fell.

The face is that of a fresh and somewhat florid man, with light-brown hair. The eye a deep clear blue, full of spirit and vivacity ; the nose resembling that of his subsequent like-nesses, but much more becoming; and the mouth indicating most emphatically that un-conquerable firmness of purpose, that inspired perseverance, that cool yet ardent character, which the history of his whole life exhibits. I should judge from this picture that Washington was naturally of a vivacious temperament, for his eye is full of fire, and its expression rather gay than grave; and I shall, in the course of this work, lay before my young readers some proofs in sup-port of my opinion. The incessant cares and labours he encountered soon after this period, and the weight of those momentous interests which so heavily lay on his mind, and would have weighed almost any other to the earth, were amply sufficient to repress this natural vivacity. Hence, from the date of his accept-ing the command in the great crusade for the establishment of the rights of his country, he was seldom known to be gay, scarcely ever laughed aloud, and his character was that of gravity, if not something more.

Washington was upwards of six feet in height; robust, but of perfect symmetry in his proportions; eminently calculated to sustain fatigue, yet without that heaviness which usually accompanies great muscular power, and abates active exertion. His movements were graceful; his manner displayed a grave self-possession, and was easy and affable. All those who ever associated with him have remarked that indescribable dignity which, though it created an affectionate confidence, at the same time repressed all freedoms, and forbade the indulgence of the slightest indecorum in his presence. His most remarkable feature was his mouth, which was perfectly unique. The lips firm and compressed. The under jaw seemed to grasp the upper with force, as if the muscles were in full action, even while he sat perfectly still and composed. Yet an air of benignity and repose always pervaded his face, and his smile displayed an extraordinary attraction. No man ever possessed in a higher degree the art, or rather the moral and physical qualifications, to ensure the respect and affection of all that came within the circle of his influence.

Such was Washington when the suffrages of his countrymen called him from his retirement, first to assist by his councils, and next to vindicate their rights in the strife of arms. While attending upon his duties as a member of the first Congress, he was, on the fourteenth of June, 1775, unanimously chosen commander-in-chief of the armies of the United Colonies, and all the forces now raised or to be raised by them. Some little effort was made in favour of General Ward of Massachusetts; but, happily for the cause and the country, local feelings and personal predilections were nobly sacrificed on the altar of patriotism, and the destinies of liberty fell upon one fully adequate to their support.

Washington accepted the dangerous pre-eminence offered him with that modest firmness which never deserted him. I have a letter before me announcing the event to Mrs. Washington, and expressing his doubts whether he is qualified for the task he had undertaken, with a simplicity that precludes all idea of affectation, if such a weakness were compatible with his character. Another, written just before his departure for Boston, to assume a command which promised little but difficulty and disaster, if not disgrace and death, I shall now lay before my young readers. It at once displays his domestic feelings, his unaffected diffidence, his uniform and affecting reliance on the goodness of Providence.

"Philadelphia, June 23d, 1775.

"My Dearest,

"As I am within a few minutes of leaving this city, I could not think of departing from it without dropping you a line, especially as I do not know whether it will be in my power to write again until I get to the camp at Boston. I go fully trusting in that Providence which has been more bountiful to me than I deserve, and in full confidence of a happy meeting with you in the fall. I have not time to add more, as I am surrounded by company to take leave of me. I retain an unalterable affection for you, which neither time or distance can change. My best love to Jack and Nelly, and regards to the rest of the family, concludes me with the utmost sincerity,

"Your entire,

"GEO. WASHINGTON."

By accepting the command of the army of the United Colonies, Washington placed his life and fortune on the issue of the struggle. He not only risked the perils of battle, which every brave man is willing to encounter in a just cause, but the imminent danger of perishing on the scaffold or under the gallows. As a leader in what was called a rebellion by the British government, the ruin of the cause of his country would, almost as a matter of course, have been followed either by a voluntary exile or an ignominious death. Indeed, my young readers ought never, while they live in the enjoyment of the blessings of liberty, to forget that those who won and transmitted them to posterity, fought, as was the reproachful phrase of their haughty antagonists, "with halters about their necks," and at the risk of perishing, as the unsuccessful champions of liberty have always perished, with the stigma of treason on their names. Under all these circumstances,

we have a right to presume, and such a conclusion accords with the whole tenor of his life,
that, in accepting a station fraught with so
many dangers and discouragements, Washington was actuated, not by the love of power,
but solely by an attachment to his country and
to the rights of his fellow-citizens.

The triumph in the cause of freedom, achieved
by the United States, as they were now soon
to be denominated, has already attracted the
admiration of nations. But they knew not half
the difficulties the good people of the colonies
had to encounter. There was a moral influence which, of itself, was almost insurmount-
able. An influence which to this day festers
in the veins of the free citizens of this independent confederation, independent in every
thing but mind. It was the influence of that
long habit of inferiority which is ever the in-
glorious birthright of colonies.

The idea of European superiority, and most
especially of British valour, British wisdom,
and, above all, British power, was an inheritance
of our forefathers, and has descended to their
children. In their eyes, England was invincible—she grasped the trident of the ocean in

one hand, and in the other the sceptre of the land. Equally pre-eminent in arms, in arts, in science, and in literature, the idea of opposing her power, or resisting her pretensions, was almost equivalent to that of the war of the pigmies against the giants. It seemed not courage, but temerity; not fortitude, but presumption; not the calm deliberate energy of freemen, determined to assert their rights, but the phrensy of a slave, gnashing his teeth, and vainly attempting to break his fetters. It was a great effort to overcome these long prepossessions, and it was reserved for the descendants of Englishmen to dissolve the charm of invincibility that had been cherished for ages in behalf of their forefathers.

Besides this soul-subduing feeling of inferiority, which generated a thousand miserable fears, there were other real and substantial grounds for all but despair. The colonies had suddenly, by the violent proceedings of the British ministry in relation to Boston, which had first dared to resist the payment of the duty on tea, been precipitated on a crisis which left them no alternative but submission or resistance. They were obliged to give up the cause, or to enter at once on its assertion by arms. Without adequate means, or unity of action, or concert of system, they had followed the impulse of a generous patriotism, which calculates no deficiencies, and flown to the relief of their brothers of New-England, on whose heads the vengeance of England had first lighted. They were too wise to wait to see their neighbours fall before they came to the rescue, and too magnanimous to desert those who were suffering in the common cause.

Washington was cheered on his way to Boston by the universal voice of confidence in the new commander; by a resolution of Congress pledging itself to stand by him with their lives and fortunes in defence of "American liberty;" by a committee which met and escorted him to Boston; and by an address presented to him by the Massachusetts House of Representatives, couched in the most respectful and affectionate language.

On entering upon the duties of his command, he soon found that, however he might rely on the spirit and patriotism of the people, the army was in a most destitute state, and afforded but small grounds for the hope of a successful issue to the struggle at hand, save through a long series of trials and suffering. There was a general defect of organization, and an almost total absence of all the munitions of war. The arms were defective, and the want of powder was a decisive obstacle to their use. The letters of Washington, from this time forward, furnish the best exposition of his situation, and the most authentic materials for a history of the difficulties, delays, and mortifications he encountered, the heroism, patience, and perseverance with which he endured or surmounted them. To them, therefore, I shall principally resort in the narrative which follows. No one can read these letters without receiving a conviction that, during the whole course of the contest for the liberties of the New World, Washington was the master spirit of the cause, and that but for his urgent solicitations to Congress; his sagacious recommendations of the measures proper to be pursued; his unwearied perseverance in stemming the tide of ill-fortune, and providing against its effects; his inflexible firmness in bearing up against every exigency; his courage, his patriotism, and his genius, all reinforced and sustained by the commanding influence of his character, the struggle of seven years might, in all probability, have been lengthened many years more—if it had not been prematurely brought to an end by the utter defeat and subjection of the States, and the postponement, if not final extinction, of all hope of independence. If ever any man merited the greatest of all titles, that of the Deliverer of his Country, it was Washington.

CHAPTER VII.

Causes of the Revolutionary War—Affair of Lexington and
Concord—Battle of Bunker's Hill—·Washington arrives at
Boston and assumes the Command—State of the American
Army—Probable Causes of the Inactivity of General Howe—
Attempt to dislodge the Americans from Dorchester Heights
—Evacuation of Boston by the British—Washington and his
Army receive the Thanks of Congress—His firm stand in be-
half of the American Prisoners, and Threat of Retaliation—
General Howe relaxes the System pursued by Governor Gage.

BEFORE entering on a detail of the actions
of Washington in the great war of the Revolution, a brief sketch of the state of affairs at that
time will be useful, to enable my youthful
readers to comprehend what follows. The dis
pute between England and her colonies origi
nated in the claim of the former to tax the
latter without their consent. They asserted
the rights of Englishmen, as the descendants
of Englishmen; and as no native of that country
could be taxed without the consent of a parliament in which he was supposed to be repre-

sented, they insisted the same rule should be extended to them. They demanded either the right of being represented in the parliament of England, or that of taxing themselves through the medium of their own colonial assemblies.

This right they always exercised, and as they had never on any occasion declined con tributing the necessary means of defraying their own expenses, and defending themselves against the Indians, and other enemies, there was no just pretext for any innovation on this long-established practice. The government of England having discovered that the colonies were growing rich, began to think them worth protecting, now that they could afford to pay for protection. Under pretence of the burden of defending them against the French and Indians in those wars which originated in the rivalry of European ambition, and in which they had no concern whatever, an act of parliament was passed laying a duty on stamps. All legal papers were obliged to bear a stamp, for which a certain sum was to be paid to certain commissioners, for the use of the British government; and, consequently, every species of business became subject to this imposition, which was equally oppressive and embarrassing.

It was not, however, the amount of the tax, nor the vexatious mode by which it was collected, that roused the resistance of the Americans. They saw that this was the commencement of a great system of imposition, founded on the supremacy of a parliament in which they were not represented, and in the choice of whose members they had no voice whatever. They saw that this was the first attempt to feel the pulse of the inhabitants of the colonies, and that submission now would be the signal for new exactions hereafter. Now, therefore, was the time to resist, or never. They must strain at the gnat or prepare themselves to swallow the camel.

Others have resisted actual oppressions; it was reserved to the Americans to wrestle for principles alone. They struggled against future rather than present evils; and, with a wisdom, firmness, and foresight to which there is no parallel example in the history of the world, met on the very threshold the enemy, which, if they had once permitted to enter the house, would have finally turned them out of doors. Their manly yet temperate remonstrances at length procured a repeal of the stamp act; but the very abandonment of the practice was accompanied by an assertion of the principle of parliamentary supremacy, on which it had been founded. The Americans continued dissatisfied with a concession which, while it abated the grievance, reserved the right to renew it whenever it was thought proper.

The frequent and expensive wars of England, which had been some time prosecuted upon the new principle of shifting on posterity the burdens of their fathers, had entailed upon that country the modern blessing of a vast national debt. This carried with it the necessity of additional taxation to meet the interest; and the British ministry began to cherish a design to make the colonies a party in contributing to the payment of debts which they had no agency in contracting. Not one of the wars of England, in which these debts were incurred, had originated in any desire to benefit he United Colonies. They were the consequences of European ambition and national rivalry.

The repeal of the stamp act was followed at no great distance of time by an attempt to collect a tax on tea, which constituted an item in the original budget of which the former was by far the most vexatious, and had never been repealed. Again was that spirit of liberty which our ancestors brought with them to the Western wilderness, and bequeathed to their posterity, roused to action. Remonstrances, petitions, and appeals, the most eloquent and unanswerable, couched in language the most respectful, were transmitted to the parliament, the people, and the king of England. All these addresses were written with a vigour, a temperate dignity, and a force of reasoning characteristic of an enlightened people determined to maintain their rights; a people whose ancestors had sought the untrodden wilds of a New World that they might escape the despotism of Church and State, and bequeathed to them an abhorrence of tyranny. That to the people of England, written by John Jay, is one of the finest productions of those times which awakened and

gave new energies to the genius and virtue of
our countrymen.   It furnishes the heads of the
principles asserted by our ancestors.

"Know then," it says, "that we consider
ourselves, and do insist that we are and ought
to be, as free as our fellow-subjects of Great
Britain, and that no power on earth has a right
to take our property from us without our
consent.

"That we claim all the benefits secured to
the subject by the English Constitution, and
particularly that inestimable one of trial by jury.
That we hold it essential to English liberty,
that no man be condemned unheard, or pun-
ished for supposed offences, without having an
opportunity of making his defence.

"That we think the Legislature of Great
Britain is not authorized by the constitution to
establish a religion fraught with sanguinary and
impious tenets, or to erect an arbitrary form of
government in any quarter of the globe. These
rights we, as well as you, deem sacred. And
yet, sacred as they are, they have, with many
others, been repeatedly and flagrantly violated.

"Are the proprietors of the soil of Great

Britain all lords of their own property? Can it be taken from them without their consent? Will they yield to the arbitrary disposal of any man or number of men whatever? You know they will not.

"Why, then, are the proprietors of the soil of America less lords of their property than you are of yours? Or why should they submit to the disposal of your parliament, or any other parliament or council in the world, not of their election? Can the intervention of the sea that divides us cause disparity in our rights? Or can any reason be given why English subjects who live three thousand miles from the royal palace should enjoy less liberty than those who are three hundred miles distant from it? Reason looks with indignation on such chimerical distinctions, and freemen can never perceive their propriety."

The people of England responded to the appeal, but had too little influence to obtain justice for their brethren across the Atlantic; the king permitted his ministers to follow out their own policy; and the parliament referred their complaints to what were aptly called "Committees

of Oblivion," where they were never heard **of**
more.

A few voices were heard in the British senate pleading the cause of the Americans. But
though among them were those of a Burke and
a Pitt, they were as voices crying in the wilderness, unheard except by stocks and stones,
and animals without sympathy.   Their appeals
in behalf of the rights of the descendants of
Englishmen fell dead to the ground, though
they would seem to have been calculated to
awaken the dead from their graves.   The elder
Pitt, who had in an hour of weakness buried
the glory of an illustrious name in the obscurity
of an empty title,* vindicated the rights of our
forefathers in a manner which entitles him to
the lasting gratitude of their posterity.

"For God's sake," said he on one occasion,
when addressing the House of Lords—"for
God's sake then, my lords, let the way be in-
stantly opened for reconciliation. I say in-
stantly, or it will be too late. The Americans
tell you—and remember it is the language of
three millions of people—they tell you they
will never submit to be taxed without their own
consent. They insist on a repeal of your laws.

---

* He had been created Earl of Chatham.

They do not ask it as a favour; they claim it as a right. They demand it. And I tell you the acts *must* be repealed—they *will* be repealed. You cannot enforce them. But the bare repeal will not satisfy this enlightened and spirited people. What! satisfy them by cancelling a bit of paper—a piece of parchment! No, my lords! you must go further; you must declare you have no right to tax them. Then they may trust you—then they will confide in you.

"There are, my lords, three millions of whigs in America. Three millions of whigs with arms in their hands, which every one knows how to use, are a formidable body. There are, I trust, twice as many whigs in England; and I hope the whigs in both countries will unite, and make a common cause in defence of their common rights. They are united by the strongest ties of sentiment and interest; and will, therefore, I hope, fly to support their brethren. In this most alarming and distracted state of your affairs, though borne down by disease, I have crawled to this house, my lords, to give you my best advice, which is, to beseech his majesty that orders may be in-stantly despatched to General Gage to remove his troops from Boston. Their presence is a source of perpetual irritation and suspicion to those people. How can they trust you with the bayonet at their breasts?

"They have all the reason in the world to believe that you mean to deal them death or slavery. Let us then set about this business in earnest. There is no time to be lost. Every moment is big with danger. Even while I am speaking, the decisive blow may be struck, and millions involved in the consequences. The very first drop of blood that is shed will make a wound perhaps never to be healed—a wound of such uncommon malignity as will never be closed. It will mortify the whole body, and hasten, both in England and America, that dissolution to which all the nations of the earth are destined."

But when were mother countries ever just to their children? The inflexible policy has ever been to make their industry tributary to their own luxury and ambition; to make them the rich pastures for foraging their own greedy dependants; to insult and harass them with indignities and restraints of every kind, and finally to leave them no alternative but slavery or resistance unto death. The voice of wisdom, justice, and patriotism—the eloquence of inspiration and virtue combined, bursting as it were from the brink of the grave, was unheard. The knife was placed at the throat of America, and the prophecy of the great statesman was fulfilled.

The immediate occasion which produced the first act of resistance on the part of the Americans was an attempt to introduce a cargo of tea into Boston, on which a duty of three-pence a pound was laid by act of parliament. Trifling as it was, it involved the whole principle of the right of taxation without representation, and the patriotic inhabitants of Boston, who had before signalized themselves on various occasions by their stern resistance to every encroachment on their rights, proceeded to settle the question in a summary manner. A party disguised as Indians entered the vessel, and threw the whole cargo overboard. Such was the admirable secrecy with which this was meditated, proposed, and performed, that though every effort was made by the royal governor and his instruments to discover the actors, not one betrayed himself, or was betrayed by the others. To this day the names of a large portion of these daring patriots remain either questionable or unknown.

When this proceeding became known in England, it called down the vengeance of the ministry and its subservient parliament on the devoted city. An act was passed shutting up the port of Boston, and of course destroying its trade entirely. Reinforcements were sent to Governor Gage, and every thing indicated a settled determination on the part of the British ministry to enforce the system of taxation. These acts roused the indignation, while they awakened the fears of the Americans. The rest of the colonies considered that Boston was suffering in the common cause, and promptly resolved to make common cause with her. The people of New-England especially took the deepest interest in the fate of their capital, and a generous excitement pervaded the whole country. A general congress of all the colonies was convened, whose first act was a Declaration of Rights, in which they asserted the ancient privileges of Englishmen, professed their loyalty to the king, and their determination " to risk every thing short of their eternal salvation to defend and transmit those rights entire to their innocent and beloved posterity." The people seconded their representatives, and agreed to an abstinence from all British manufactures, which then constituted nearly all their luxuries and most of their comforts.

In this state of affairs a spark fell among the combustibles and lighted the flames of a seven-years war. Congress had ordered a deposite of stores and ammunition at Concord, a village about thirteen miles from Boston. Governor Gage despatched a force of eight hundred grenadiers and light infantry for the purpose of destroying them. Information having been sent by Doctor Warren, one of the early martyrs in the cause of freedom, the inhabitants of Concord and its vicinity prepared for the reception of the enemy.

Arriving at Lexington, the British met a party of about twenty militia and thirty or forty unarmed spectators. Major Pitcairn, who commanded the former, rode up to them, and cried out, in a furious tone, " Disperse, you rebels— lay down your arms and disperse." This in sulting command not being promptly obeyed, he discharged his pistol, and ordered his men to fire. He was immediately obeyed, and the inhabitants fled, while the British continued their fire. This at length provoked resistance; the inhabitants returned the fire, and several were killed on both sides.

The British continued to advance on Concord. The news of the affair at Lexington had spread like fire on a prairie through the neighbourhood, and roused a spirit of resistance. Armed men seemed to spring out of the earth; the farmers left their ploughs sticking in the furrows, and the horses in their gears, and seizing their muskets, rushed to the defence of their country. Intimidated, however, by the number of the enemy, they took a position behind a bridge, and waited for reinforcements, while the British proceeded to destroy the stores and ammunition.

Having done this, they marched upon the bridge to disperse the militia. They again gave the first fire, which was returned with such effect that they were compelled to retreat. They were pursued by the Americans; who, now roused to vengeance, no longer stood on the defensive.   As they fled towards Boston, it was like running the gauntlet.   The woods, the windows, and the stone fences were alive with irritated freemen, and every shot made its mark on the enemy.   The ball rolled, and gathered as it rolled ; and before the enemy returned to Boston, two hundred and seventy-three, in killed, wounded, and prisoners, had paid the forfeit of shedding the first blood in the cause of oppression.

The inhabitants of Lexington, Concord, and the neighbouring country, proved themselves on this occasion worthy descendants of the pious and gallant pilgrims, who had sacrificed all for liberty in the Old World, and braved, in the same cause, the dangers, hardships, and privations of the New. Of the company of volunteer militia belonging to Lexington, seven were killed and ten wounded.   It seems to have been a family of brothers, for among them were nine of the name of Smith, twelve of Harrington, and thirteen, one for each of the states, of Munroe.

The name of every man belonging to the little band which furnished the first martyrs to liberty in this western world, should be re-

ꜱorded and remembered. The anniversary of
.he battle of Lexington deserves to be kept, and
has lately been commemorated in a manneɪ
equally honourable to the living and the dead ,
and long may it be before the children or the
men of my country become indifferent to the
heroism and sacrifices of their humble ances
tors.

On this occasion there occurred instances ɔf
devoted and persevering courage which may,
and ought to be, placed side by side with any
that adorn the history of Greece and Rome.
The following will serve as one among many
examples. It is that of Jonas Parker. "He
had been heard to say that, be the consequences what they might, and let others do as
they pleased, he would never run from the en
emy. He was as good as his word—better.
Having loaded his musket, he placed his hat,
containing his ammunition, on the ground between his feet, in readiness for a second charge.
At the second fire he was wounded, and sunk
on his knees ; and in this condition discharged
his gun. While loading it again upon his
knees, and striving in the agonies of death to
redeem his pledge, he was transfixed by a bay

onet, and thus died on the spot where he stood and fell."* While my youthful readers glow with affecting admiration over such examples of courage and patriotism in the lowly village train, let them receive them as lessons of what they themselves will owe to their beneficent country, should it ever again require such sacrifices.

I have dwelt the more particularly on this affair because of the momentous consequences which followed. Trifling as it appears in itself, it was of greater magnitude in its results than many battles and wars in which empires were laid waste, and millions perished by the sword. It was the first link in a chain of circumstances that drew after it the fate of the New, perhaps of the Old World. It was the first sentence of a chapter which records the downfall of oppression, and the commencement of a new era in the history of mankind. The course of human affairs ; the great change which is now daily operating on the despotism of power, and the rights of nations ; the revolution of opinions, of governments, and of

* I quote from the fine address of Mr. Edward **Everett in** commemoration of this battle

things, all derived a beginning from the fields of Lexington and Concord. There was shed the blood of the first martyrs to liberty, and from thence she dates her new-born existence.

The famous battle of Bunker Hill followed at no great distance, and formed the second act of the great drama. A second time the kindred blood of the two people who had once been friends and brothers, flowed in the same strife of principle on the one hand, power on the other; there was the gallantry of the assailant met by more than equal firmness of resistance; and there upwards of thirteen hundred of the royal army paid a second forfeit to their contempt of those whom they denominated rebels to their king, because they refused to be bond-slaves to his ministers. The invaders here learned another lesson, which taught them that those who are animated by a love of liberty are never to be despised.

The battle of Bunker Hill, by which name it was first known, and will be longest remembered, is equally memorable for the gallantry displayed on both sides, as for its impressive influence on the events which followed. It taught the enemy caution, and inspired the

Americans with confidence. The place is not strong by nature, nor had the militia, who took possession, time to throw up any other defences except a ditch of moderate depth and dimensions and a paltry breastwork. They had neither cannon nor bayonets, and depended on their skill as marksmen, their courage as the champions of a good cause.

They had taken possession of the hill by night, and as soon as the light of the dawn enabled Governor Gage to see that they were there, a cannonade from his ships of war was directed to dislodge them : but they stood their ground, and continued their work. Three thousand men, with a train of artillery, under Howe and Pigot, were then landed near Charlestown, which, in order as it would seem to exasperate the Americans to a more determined resistance, they set fire to, and laid in ashes. They then formed, and advanced towards the hill, while the American and British armies, and the inhabitants of Boston, were watching the result in breathless expectation. Here was to be the first trial whether the posterity of Englishmen had degenerated in the New World, and the event was to decide whether they were worthy the . liberty they were now about to assert.

On the brow of the hill stood the Americans in their little intrenchment, watching with eyes that never winked, and hearts that never quailed, the approach of that enemy whom they were brought up to believe invincible. Their supply of ammunition being exceedingly scarce, they were directed to reserve their fire till the last moment. The brave "Old Putnam," as he is called with affectionate license by a grateful people, ordered them not to throw away a single shot, nor to touch a trigger till they could see "the whites of their eyes."

The gallant British soldiers, for gallant they were, came steadily on, silent as the grave so many of them were soon to occupy, and were waited for by a foe equally silent. Not a word was spoken within the American line of defence; every man was marking out, with unerring aim, the victim who, instead of imagining he was advancing to his fate, dreamed that he should meet no resistance. But from this dream he was awakened by the messenger of death. Soon as the whites of their eyes became visible a thousand triggers snapped, and a thousand muskets at one single discharge, that made but one report, arrested the career of the whole body, a considerable portion of it for ever. The British halted for a moment, keeping up an irregular fire, and receiving others more deadly and unerring. They fell like armies smitten by the angel of death; but those who escaped stood their ground manfully, maintaining the ancient renown of their country even in a bad cause. But the deadly fire was continued so rapidly, and with such horrible effects, that the commands of the officers were no longer heard or obeyed. They broke in confusion, and precipitated themselves down the hill. Again they were rallied; again they were met by the same deadly and determined fire, and again they were broken, and retreated down the hill. Fresh troops were sent to their assistance by those who were watching the conflict; and once more, with a perseverance and intrepidity, the result equally perhaps of an arrogant presumption of their own superiority, and a contempt for their enemy—once more they advanced with all the courage of desperation. But by this time the occupants of this immortal little breastwork had expended all their am munition, with the exception of a few rounds, and they retreated in as good order as could be expected from irregular troops, after firing their last cartridge, and dealing a last blow with the butt-ends of their muskets.

The enemy at length gained the victory, but at a price which perhaps led him to calculate the cost of a contest that had thus commenced. Instead of songs of triumph there was weeping and gnashing of teeth for breathless friends and comrades, or living sufferers, some without limbs, others pierced through the body, others bloodless as shivering ghosts. It was a sorrowful day for England, for she had lost many brave soldiers, many gallant officers, and gained no honour. The wages of so much slaughter were but a ditch and breastwork on the summit of a little hill. For this, thirteen hundred and upwards of the enemy paid the price of their breath or their blood. The loss of the Americans was serious, yet by no means to be compared to that of the British. Among the killed was Dr. Joseph Warren, a distinguished volunteer, whose death was deeply lamented ; and who, had Providence spared him to the cause of his country, would, without doubt, have become one of the first among those that survived him.   But his death was glorious, and his name will ever be quoted as that of one of the earliest as well as most illustrious of the martyrs to the liberties of his native land.

These two affairs of Lexington and Bunker Hill appertain exclusively to New-England. It was on New-England ground, and by the men of New-England these battles were fought, for as yet the more distant colonies had not time to come to the aid of their brothers of the East. They constitute bright pages in the history of those states, most especially of Massachusetts, fortunate in being the first to be attacked, the first to resist, and the first to seal the charter of liberty with her blood.   Truth demands this testimony, and the honour should neither be envied nor withheld.

Though the mother country had actually commenced hostilities, and the colonies resisted, still there are many clear indications in the history of those times that, until a considerable period after the American Congress had recommended and authorized strong measures of defence, few, if any, cherished the idea that the British ministers would persevere in enforcing the claims of England to absolute **su-premacy** after they found that the colonies were determined to resist at all hazards.

On the other hand, the British ministry laboured under a similar delusion. They imagined that the colonies had neither the spirit to resist, nor the power to do it effectually. They calculated securely on the long habits of deference which had grown up among them, their attachment to the country of their descent, and their apprehensions of its vengeance. They were taught to believe—for it is the destiny of power to be always deceived—that the mere show of a resolution to enforce it would produce a prompt obedience. They deceived themselves, and suffered the consequences of the deception. They plunged boldly into the stream, and their pride prohibited returning when they discovered the force of the current. Had they foreseen the difficulty of the task, it is highly probable they would have at least temporized, if not abandoned it altogether. But even this would not have answered their purpose. It was the destiny of the New World to become independent of the Old, and nothing could **have** finally prevented its accomplishment.

On the 12th of June, 1775, Governor Gage is sued a proclamation declaring the colony of Massachusetts in a state of rebellion; threatening the severest punishment to the insurgents; and proffering pardon on submission to all, with the honourable exception of Samuel Adams and John Hancock.

When Washington arrived at the lines of the American army before Boston, in the beginning of July, 1775, he found the situation of affairs by no means promising, and now commenced that correspondence with the president of Congress, the celebrated John Hancock, from which I shall draw my principal materials. It corroborates the view above taken, when I observe that in all his early letters he calls the British the "ministerial army," thus avoiding a direct collision with the authority of the king.

His first acts were to visit the several posts and reconnoitre those of the enemy. His second, to ascertain the situation of his army, and the means of offensive or defensive operations in his power. The results of the latter inquiry were sufficiently discouraging.

The deficiencies consisted in a want of en

gineers ; a want of arms ; of ammunition; of tents ; of regular supplies of provisions ; of a military chest, that is to say, of money ; and, indeed, of almost every necessary constituent of a military force and military action, except "a great number of able-bodied men, zealous in the cause, and of unquestionable courage." He earnestly recommends to Congress a prompt attention to these objects, and laments the distance of that body, which impedes a direct and frequent communication.

"My best abilities," he writes, "are at all times devoted to the service of my country. But I feel the weighty importance and variety of my present duties too sensibly not to wish a more frequent communication with Congress. I fear it may often happen, in the course of our present operations, that I shall need that assistance and direction from them which time and distance will not allow me to receive."

Thus in a situation where ambitious and aspiring men grasp at discretionary power, and sigh to be free from the restraints of legislative supervision, in order that they may follow the dictates of their own will, or perhaps usurp the liberties of the state, did Washington regret the want of a superintending authority. Through-out the whole of the struggle for liberty he never, on any occasion, attempted to interfere with the civil power, or to transcend the func-tions delegated to him by Congress. He con-sidered himself only as the servant of the state and sought no other distinction, although con-tinually placed in circumstances that might have justified the exercise of almost unlimited discretion.

But at the same time he neither cringed nor flattered. He never failed to give his own opin-ions frankly ; to point out to Congress what he considered proper or necessary to the com-fort of his soldiers or the success of their ope-rations, and to blame, with a temperate manli-ness, its neglect or inertness. His intimations are succeeded by remonstrances, and his re-monstrances are repeated with a firm, yet re-spectful importunity, until the evil is remedied, or all hope of remedy abandoned.

After the battle of Bunker Hill, no action of any consequence took place at Boston. Wash-ington, though exceedingly anxious to storm the British lines, was deterred by a want of the necessary means, and the decision of a

council of officers, disapproving such an a
tempt.   Great difficulties took place in the
mean time in consequence of the expiration of
the term of enlistment of a large portion of the
troops ; the different organization of those of
the different states, which precluded uniformity;
together with the want of habits of subordina-
tion in both officers and soldiers, who, while
struggling for civil liberty, did not sufficiently
comprehend the necessity of submitting to the
severity of a military code.

These difficulties were increased by local
jealousies among the troops of the different colonies, which, while they produced, perhaps, a
salutary emulation on the one hand, occasioned on
the other feelings directly opposed to a harmo-
nious co-operation.   To remedy this, in some
degree, Washington proposed to Congress that
the whole army should be dressed in hunting-
shirts, which, while they furnished a cheap uniform, would do away with those petty dissen
sions which have often no better foundation
than a different coloured coat or feather.   The
naterial for this arrangement could not, however, be procured, and the recommendation
was, consequently, not carried into effect.

On the other hand, the British, who occupied Boston and its immediate defences, remained comparatively quiet within their intrenchments. It is not possible that General Howe, who commanded under Governor Gage, and afterwards succeeded him, was ignorant of the total want of a supply of ammunition under which the Americans laboured for a considerable time. Indeed, Washington explicitly states, in one of his letters to Congress, that this deficiency was known in the enemy's camp, and expresses his surprise at the inactivity of Howe. I am strongly inclined to believe it was in a great measure owing to his expectation of a speedy adjustment of the quarrel between the mother country and her colonies, and a desire not to increase the difficulty of such an arrangement by additional bloodshed.

The only effort made by General Howe against the Americans who were investing Boston, was to dislodge them from Dorchester Heights, which had been taken possession of by General Thomas. A party of three thousand British under Lord Percy were sent on this errand, but a furious storm arrested their vessels in the passage to the mouth of the river up which they were to proceed to the point of action; and before they could repair damages, the Americans had so strengthened their works that the attempt to carry them by storm was abandoned.

The possession of these heights rendered the situation of the enemy not a little critical, and produced a determination on the part of General Howe to evacuate Boston without any further attempt at defence. This resolution was carried into effect the 17th of March, 1776, and Boston at length reposed in the arms, and under the protection, of its natural defenders. This event was hailed with triumph and rejoicing throughout the whole extent of the united colonies, where the cause of Boston was identified with their best principles and most ardent affections. A medal was ordered to be struck by Congress to commemorate the event, and a vote of thanks passed, in which the conduct of Washington and his army is justly characterized as equally "wise and spirited." It was indeed a rational source of exultation, to drive an invading army from its intrenchments with a force comparatively raw, undisciplined, and ill-supplied with every thing. The act was glorious, and the consequences in the highest degree important. It freed a patriotic and devoted city; it gave additional confidence to the friends of liberty, and held forth bright omens of future successes, should the struggle continue.

The conduct of Washington was universally approved by the friends of the good cause. His temperate ardour, exhibited on all occasions in seeking the delivery of the city; the firmness yet kind forbearance with which he had dealt with the feelings of the troops under his command, who had suffered much, and were unused to the hardships and discipline of war; and, in short, his whole deportment had been such as to justify his past reputation, and lay the solid, unshaken basis of that confidence in his vigour, firmness and integrity which supported him in all the future trials of his country.

It was here too that he took a stand from which he never swerved, until the British were taught by his firmness, and perseverance to abandon a system of treating their prisoners equally cruel and insulting. They either did, or affected to look on the noble struggle for liberty, which has since been consecrated by the admiration and imitation of many nations, as nothing more than a petulent and ungrateful opposition to long-established authority. While a large portion of the people of England sympathized in the wrongs of the colonies, the ministry and the soldiers considered them as rebellious subjects, in arms against their king without cause, and without justice. With this impression they treated their prisoners with an insulting and reckless barbarity, which under no circumstances could be justified among civilized nations. They pretended to consider them as without the pale of honourable warfare, and abused them as they would the worst of criminals. They placed them in irons, and threatened them with the gallows.

Washington wrote to Governor Gage, remonstrating against this barbarity. A haughty and supercilious answer was returned, in which it was intimated that an escape from the halter was all the prisoners could expect; and for this clemency they should be grateful, instead of complaining of their benefactors. To this Washington replied, " If your officers, our pris·oners, receive from me treatment different from that I wished to show them, they and you wil remember the occasion." Soon after, the command devolved on General Howe, who, either from a conviction that his severity would be retaliated, or from a better motive, for some time afterwards adopted a milder course towards his prisoners.

CHAPTER VIII.

Character of the War—The British evacuate Boston, and Washington proceeds to New-York—State of Affairs there—Declaration of Independence—Arrival of Lord Howe at Sandy Hook—Sends a Flag with Proposals for Conciliation—Lands on Long Island—Battle, and Defeat of the Americans—Fine Retreat of Washington—This ill Success does not impair the Public Confidence in him—Abortive Meeting of a Committee of Congress with Lord Howe, and Rejection of his Offers of Pardon.

THE war which Washington was now conducting was not one of brilliant victories, rousing the unthinking admiration of mankind by the mass of human misery they create, but of difficulties and disasters, calling for the exercise of all the highest qualities of mind and genius to surmount. These alone enabled him to support the labours and vanquish the obstacles that, wherever he went, bristled thick in his way, and, by the blessing of Heaven, to secure a lasting and glorious triumph to the cause of liberty.

The moment he perceived by the motions of General Howe that the British army was preparing to leave Boston, Washington commenced breaking up his camp at Cambridge, and was soon on his way to New-York, whither, he believed, the enemy would direct his course ere long, although, on leaving Nantasket Roads, he had sailed eastward. He passed through Providence, Norwich, and New-London, and everywhere directed his attention to the arduous duties devolved upon him as commander-in-chief. He provided for the embarkation of his army at New-London; sent a reinforcement to the American troops in Canada; procured a small supply of cannon from Admiral Hopkins at New-London; and, in short, devoted his time and energies to preparing for the worst that might happen. Everywhere he exerted the influence of his personal character, and everywhere with the most beneficial consequences. It was this influence, arising from a perfect confidence in his talents, integrity, and patriotism, that more than once proved the bulwark and safeguard of his country.

On his arrival at New-York early in the

month of April, 1776, he received a letter from the President of Congress conveying the thanks of that body to himself and his army for their conduct at the siege of Boston. He replied with his usual modest manliness—" I beg you," he says, " to assure them, that it will ever be my highest ambition to approve myself a faithful servant of the public; and that to be in any degree instrumental in procuring for my American brethren a restitution of their just rights and privileges will constitute my chief happiness." Speaking of having communicated the thanks of Congress to the army, he adds, " They were indeed at first a band of undisciplined husbandmen, but it is, under God, to their bravery and attention to their duty that I am indebted for that success which has procured me the only reward I wish to receive, the affection and esteem of my countrymen."

Washington found New-York but ill-prepared for defence in the event of General Howe's directing his operations to that quarter. The state troops were deficient in arms, and many of the citizens equally deficient in pa triotism. Owing to various causes, the tory influence was strong in that quarter. A con

siderable number of British troops were always
stationed in New-York; the officers had many
of them intermarried with the most influential
families of the province; and a number of the
proprietors of the largest estates were devoted
loyalists. Add to this, the Asia, man-of-war,
lay opposite the city for some time, having it
entirely at her mercy, and the commander
threatening destruction in case of any overt act
of opposition to the mother country.

These and other causes damped the efforts
of the whigs, and delayed decisive measures
of defence. But the body of the people
was sound. The "Sons of Liberty," as they
styled themselves, and who represented the
popular feeling, had finally obtained the as-
cendency over their disaffected opponents, and
aided by a body of troops from Connecticut,
under General Lee, maintained possession of
the city in defiance of the threats of the commander of the Asia. That officer declared that
if any troops came into the city, he would set
it on fire; and Lee replied—"that if he set
fire to a single house in consequence of his
coming, he would chain a hundred tories to-

gether by the neck, and make that house their funeral pile."

The possession of New-York, the key to the Hudson, which forms the great geographical line of separation between New-England and the South, and is, moreover, the most direct route to and from Canada, was deemed an object of the first importance. Accordingly, Washington used his utmost efforts to place it in the best possible state of defence. At his recommendation, Congress authorized the con struction of such a number of rafts calculated to act as a sort of fire-ships, armed boats, row-galleys, and floating-batteries as were deemed necessary to the command of the port and river. They likewise voted the employment of thirteen thousand militia, to reinforce the main army under Washington.

Hitherto the Americans had been simply struggling for their rights as subjects of England; but the time had now arrived when the contest was to assume an entirely different character. An event was at hand which was to change the relations between the mother coun try and her colonies, and separate their future destinies for ever. The assertion of rights had

produced the desire of independence.   To the
more sagacious of that great and illustrious
body of men which composed the first Congress, it gradually became evident that, though
the ancient relations of the two countries might
perhaps be revived for a time, there never could
in future subsist that cordiality which was in
dispensable to their mutual interests and happi
ness.   Blood had been shed ; bitter invectives
and biting insults had been exchanged ; injuries
never to be forgotten, and outrages not to be
forgiven, had been suffered ; and the filial piety
of the children had been turned into hatred of
the tyranny of the mother.

They saw, too, that were England to relin
quish her claim to parliamentary supremacy for
the present, there would be no security for the
future.   The colonies would be left as before,
equally exposed to a revival and enforcement
of the obnoxious claim of taxation without rep
resentation.   Union could no longer subsist
compatibly with the mutual happiness of the
two parties, and a separation became the only
security against eternal family strife.   The
lofty pride of patriotism, which disdains to
wear the yoke even of those we have been ac

customed to reverence, when it presses too heavily, came in aid of these considerations, and enforced the only just and rational conclusion.

Actuated by these high motives, on the 7th of June, 1776, Richard Henry Lee consecrated his name to the everlasting gratitude of his country, by a motion in the Congress of the United Colonies that a declaration of independence should be adopted. Three days after the question was taken up, and postponed to the first of July; but in the mean time, Thomas Jefferson of Virginia, John Adams of Massachusetts, Benjamin Franklin of Pennsylvania, Roger Sherman of Connecticut, and Robert R. Livingston of New-York, were appointed a committee to draft the proposed declaration. The day being come, the subject was taken up, the declaration read, and the most important question that ever did, or ever can arise in this country settled for ever, by the adoption of that famous Declaration of Independence which has become the political decalogue of all who love and strive for the maintenance or recovery of their rights.

Time has disclosed that this noble paper was

written by Thomas Jefferson of Virginia, who, had he done nothing else for his fame, and conferred no other obligation on his country, would deserve to be remembered in all future time, and venerated by all posterity. It was a noble sight to see this body of illustrious patriots listening to the reading of a declaration of injuries, ending with an eternal abjuration of the authority which inflicted them; to a proposition to divorce one world from another; to one of the most able and eloquent expositions of the rights of nature and nations that ever flowed from the pen of man. It was a sight still more solemn and affecting to see them, with steady hand and unshaken purpose, one after another signing their names to a paper which might have been equally their death-warrant as their patent of immortality, and solemnly pledging themselves to an act by which each one placed in the deepest jeopardy " his life, his fortune, and his sacred honour," for had they failed of success each one would have died the death of a traitor. Nor is it among the least of the attributes of sublimity by which this scene is surrounded, that, of the committee which thus cut asunder for ever the ties which had for ages cemented two countries, of which the past history of the one is but the shadow of the future glories of the other, one was bred a shoemaker, another a printer. It is thus my young readers may learn that no station in life, however high, confers a monopoly of either talents or virtue ; and that, on the other hand, no situation, however humble, can effectually repress the energies of their heaven-inspired possessors. Neither rank, nor birth, nor wealth, nor power can give dignity to weakness or vice ; nor can any depression of fortune strip genius and virtue united, of their claim to direct, under Providence, the destinies of mankind.

On the eighth of July following, the declaration was read at the State-house in Philadelphia, and received with acclamations. It was also read to each of the brigades of those troops which now assumed the proud title of the army of the United States, who received it with equal enthusiasm. Henceforward they were to fight under the banner, not of England, but of independence ; not of the red cross, but the stripes and stars. They were now emphatically the soldiers of freedom, and their courage increased with the consciousness of their new dignity. Now it was that every one became sensible that he was contending for the noblest of prizes ; and now it was that the souls of all true lovers of liberty were put to the test. Many, who had hitherto gone hand in hand in the assertion of the principle of taxation and representation, shrunk from the idea of an assertion of entire independence on the mother country. They were either too much attached to " home," as England was usually called, or they feared the consequences of the long struggle that seemed now inevitable. They believed that the British ministry might have been wrought upon by the resistance of the colonies to relinquish their system of taxation, but they despaired of their ever consenting to acknowledge the independence of the States.

The first years of the new-born child of liberty were those of danger and suffering. Her cradle was assailed by the serpent, but she proved the sister of Hercules, and slew him at last. She was nurtured in bloody strife and cruel vicissitudes, but she grew only the wiser and stronger for the buffeting of the waves and the violence of the storm. Like the oak in the whirlwind, she became only the more deeply rooted in the soil of freedom from the energy with which she withstood its lashings.

Four days after the declaration of independence was read to the troops, the fleet of Lord Howe, bringing a force of upwards of twenty-five thousand men, entered the Narrows, between Long and Staten Islands, and anchored opposite. This was an army of veterans, commanded by officers inured to service, and supplied with every requisite for prompt and decisive action. To oppose them the Americans mustered, rank and file, about seventeen thousand, most of them of little experience, commanded by officers equally inexperienced, and deficient in arms, as well as every other necessary of war. But they were animated by a just sense of their rights, and an inflexible resolution to maintain them.

The first act of Lord Howe was directed towards a reconciliation between the contending parties. He sent a flag of truce ashore with circular letters to some of the old royal governors, enclosing a declaration announcing his authority to grant pardons "to all who would return to their allegiance in proper time." These were transmitted to Congress by Washington, and directed to be published for the information of the people. His lordship at or near the same time sent a letter, directed to George Washington, Esquire, affecting thus to deny his claim to the title of commander-in-chief of the armies of the United States. Washington declined receiving it, saying that it was only in that character he could have intercourse with Lord Howe. Congress very properly approved this dignified proceeding.

Soon after this Colonel Patterson was deputed by Lord Howe to confer with the American general on the subject of the settlement of all differences, but without success. "I find," said Washington, "you are only empowered to grant pardons; we have committed no offence, we need no pardon." Colonel Patterson returned with this answer, and both parties prepared for active determined war.

The twenty-second day of August, in the second month of our independence, the enemy landed on Long Island, with a design to approach New-York in that quarter. Washington had the wisdom to know that the fears of inexperience almost always overshoot the mark; and that men are most apprehensive

of those dangers of which they have least knowledge. He knew that the only way to make
soldiers out of raw recruits was to accustom
them to facing the enemy. The inexperienced
soldier goes into action expecting certain death,
and a few escapes cause him to imagine himself little less than invulnerable. Waiting for
the enemy never increases the courage of an
army, and it is better to be sometimes beaten
than to be always running away.

Influenced by these considerations perhaps,
and certainly by a desire to save New-York, as
he had regained Boston, Washington distributed
his force to such points as were most accessi-
ble to the enemy, and most easily defended.
A portion was stationed on Long Island, to
make a stand in the event of General Howe
landing in that quarter. The remainder, with
the exception of a part of the militia of New-
York, which lay at New-Rochelle, were disposed at different points of York Island, in an-
ticipation that the enemy might approach by
the way of Kingsbridge.

In this state of things every appearance in
dicated that a battle was to be fought ere long,
and that its issue would, in all probability, de

cide the fate of the most important position in the United States. Washington prepared for the crisis with courage and sagacity. Far from sanguine, yet he did not despair of success, though every way inferior to the British. Speaking of his soldiers, he says, " The superiority of the enemy and the expected attack does not seem to have depressed their spirits. These considerations lead me to think that, though the appeal may not terminate so happily as I could wish, yet that the enemy will not succeed in their views without considerable loss. Any advantage they may gain I trust will cost them dear."

Besides performing the duties of a careful and skilful soldier, he used every effort to animate and inspire those under his command. He appealed to their courage and their patriotism; to their sense of the wrongs of their country; to their recollections of the past, and their hopes of the future. In the general orders addressed to them on the arrival of Lord Howe, he says :—" The time is now near at hand which must determine whether Americans are to be freemen or slaves; whether they are to have any property they can call their own;

whether their houses and farms are to be pillaged and destroyed, and themselves consigned to a state of wretchedness from which no human efforts will deliver them. The fate of unborn millions will now depend, under God, on the courage and conduct of this army. Our cruel and unrelenting enemy leaves us only the choice of a brave resistance or the most abject submission. We have therefore to resolve to conquer or to die. Our own, our country's honour, call upon us for a vigorous exertion, and if we now shamefully fail we shall become infamous to the whole world. Let us then rely on the goodness of our cause, and the aid of the Supreme Being, in whose hands is victory to animate and encourage us to noble actions. The eyes of all our country are now upon us, and we shall have their blessings and praises if happily we become the instruments of saving them from the tyranny meditated against them. Let us therefore animate and encourage each other, and show the whole world that a freeman contending for liberty on his own ground is superior to any slavish mercenary on earth."

Again, as the hour approached, he once more endeavoured to infuse into his army a portion of his own energy and enthusiasm. "The enemy's whole force is now arrived, so that an attack must and will soon be made. The general therefore again repeats his earnest request that every officer and soldier will have his arms and ammunition in good order; keep within his quarters and encampments as far as possible; be ready for action at a moment's call; and when called, remember that liberty, property, life, and honour, are all at stake; that upon their courage and conduct rest the hopes of their bleeding country; that their wives, children, and parents expect safety from them only, and that we have every reason to believe that Heaven will crown with success so just a cause."

At length, on the 22d of August, 1776, the greater portion of the British army, under the direction of Sir Henry Clinton, landed on Long Island, and disposed itself in a line extending from the Narrows to the village of Flatlands. The troops under General Sullivan, on the island, were now reinforced by six regiments, under General Putnam, who was directed to take command at Brooklyn, and guard all the approaches by every means in his power. The two armies were now divided by the range of hills called Brooklyn Heights, and within three or four miles of each other. The British superior in numbers, equipment, and discipline, and confident of success; the soldiers of freedom fighting under every disadvantage except that of a good cause.

Under cover of the darkness Sir Henry Clinton advanced with the van of his army to seize on the passes of the heights, and, favoured by the obscurity of the night, fell in with, and completely surprised and captured the American force which was to have guarded the approach. This incident was decisive, in all probability, of the action which followed. Hearing that the pass was entirely without defence, it was immediately taken possession of, and opened to the whole division a passage to the country between the heights and the East River. In the mean time General Grant, with another body of the British, advanced by a different road, skirmishing with the outposts of the Americans. This induced General Putnam to send reinforcements to that quarter; Lord Stirling led two regiments to meet the enemy towards the Narrows; General Sullivan conducted a strong

detachment towards Flatbush, while a third oc
cupied a position between that and the village
of Bedford.

It was now break of day, and the action
commenced with a brisk cannonade on both
sides, between the troops under Grant and
Stirling. In another direction De Heister and
Sullivan were engaged, and to increase the perplexity of the Americans, the British fleet began a tremendous fire on the battery at Red
Hook. This was followed, within an hour or
two, by the approach of Sir Henry Clinton on
the left of the Americans, and by a firing in the
direction of Bedford, which, by indicating the
advance of the enemy in that quarter, alarmed
the Americans with the idea of being entirely
surrounded. Thus circumstanced, great confusion began to prevail among them; and after
standing their ground as long as could be ex
pected under such circumstances, they broke
in all directions, some seeking a retreat in
the woods, and others under cover of the
works erected on Brooklyn Heights. In this
action the Americans lost nearly five hundred in killed and wounded, and upwards of one
thousand prisoners, among whom were three

general officers. It was a severe lesson, and taught them that the price of liberty, as well as every other great blessing, is in proportion to its value.

The situation of the republican army was now such as to call for the most prompt and decisive measures. On one hand they were shut in by a broad, deep, and rapid stream, on the other by a victorious army, waiting only for the dawn of morning to attack them in their weak defences. Washington, who had passed over to Long Island during the battle, called a council of war, in which it was resolved to attempt a retreat, before the wind permitted the British fleet to enter the East River, and thus render it all but impossible.

The evening came, and the night set in with a strong wind, which made it impracticable to cross in the boats provided for that purpose, and the delay of a few hours would bring day light and destruction. They felt as if standing on the brink of fate, ready to fall at every moment. Their enemies were so near that they could hear them at work with their pickaxes and shovels just without the lines, and distinguish the word of command given by the officers in the loud tones of a triumphant enemy. At length the wind changed to a gentle breeze from the southwest, accompanied by a thick fog, which added deeply to the obscurity of the night. The army, like speechless shadows, entered the boats in deathlike silence, one by one, and in such perfect order, that the whole, together with the greater part of the heavy cannon, all the field-pieces, provisions, horses, wagons, and ammunition, were in perfect safety before the British discovered that the American lines had been evacuated.

The Americans were not yet landed at New-York, when the fog which so providentially favoured their departure clearing away, discovered the British taking possession of the spot they had abandoned but half an hour before. Such was the narrow escape they had; for if the enemy had again attacked them in their present decreased numbers, and under all the disadvantages of the previous defeat, it is extremely probable that a blow might have been given that would have taken years, perhaps ages, to recover.

The result of this affair did not impair the confidence either of the troops or the nation in their general. In this, as on every occasion of his life, his fame depended not on victory or defeat. His countrymen estimated him by the just standard of his indefatigable exertions, his unquestioned integrity, his acknowledged talents, and his long-tried patriotism, not by his successes; and not even ill-fortune could injure his reputation. This was always justly ascribed to a deficiency in the means of success, and not in the leader. Such is the inestimable value of long-established character, and such its vast influence over the feelings and opinions of mankind. The success or failure of every man's fortune is decisively swayed by the general estimation of his fellow-beings, and he stands or falls by that alone. The most despotic tyrant is dependant, more or less, on public opinion.

The conduct of Lord Howe after this victory seems to confirm the opinion I have before stated, that his inactivity was the result of policy. He followed it up, not by pursuing his advantage, but by opening a negotiation for peace. General Sullivan, who had been made prisoner at the battle of Long Island, was sent on his parole to Philadelphia with a message desiring a conference on the part of the royalist chief with some of the members of Congress, as he could not treat with it as a body. After some hesitation this proposal was acceded to, and Franklin, Adams, and Rutledge deputed to receive the communication alluded to in the message of General Sullivan. Without entering on the particulars of the conference, it will be sufficient to say that it proved entirely abortive. The republicans refused to be pardoned, and the royalist general having nothing else to offer, expressed his regrets, and ended the discussion.

CHAPTER IX.

Gloomy State of Affairs—Conduct of Washington—Operations
on York Island, and in Westchester County—Capture of
Fort Washington, and Retreat of the Americans into New-
Jersey—Ill treatment of the American Prisoners—Barbarities
of the Hessians—Congress not to be blamed for depending at
first on the Militia—Caution, firmness, and perseverance of
Washington—Retreats to Trenton—Proclamation of Amnesty
by Lord Howe—Battle of Trenton—Critical Situation of
Washington—Brilliant Affair at Princeton, and its Consequences—The Armies retire to Winter-quarters.

THE cause of freedom was shrouded in darkness and gloom after the defeat of its supporters
on Long Island. The militia were discouraged,
and began to be impatient to return to their
homes. Every appearance now indicated either
the speedy subjugation of America, or a long,
lingering, and disastrous struggle, of doubtful
issue. The royal army had taken possession
of New-York soon after the battle, and a great
fire had laid a large portion of the city in ruins.
The army of Washington was decreasing in
numbers and spirit every day. The system

of colonial government had been entirely broken
up, and none other established in its place.
The new states were like children suddenly invested with the responsibilities of self-govern-
ment, without the experience requisite for the
purpose; and the internal affairs of the different
communities were directed in a great measure
by Committees of Safety, the limits of whose
powers were scarcely defined, and whose authority the people were under no legal obligation to obey. In almost any other country
anarchy would have been the result of this condition of things; but the virtue, intelligence,
and patriotism of the people saved the state,
and the love of liberty supplied the place of an
established government.

Unawed by these difficulties, and supported
by Heaven and his own unconquerable zeal in
the cause of freedom, Washington met the
crisis as he had always met, and continued to
meet, disaster and difficulties. He rose with
the occasion which demanded his exertions,
and was never so great as when he stood surrounded by ruin. Finding it hopeless to attempt
the protection of a city, a considerable number
of whose most wealthy inhabitants were disaf-

fected to the cause, with an army so entirely inferior in numbers, discipline, and equipments of
all kinds, Washington evacuated New-York, and
took his station on the strong grounds about
Kingsbridge, which he fortified at all points,
so far as his limited time and means would
permit.

In order to surround him in this position,
General Howe, leaving a portion of his army in
New-York, proceeded by water to Throg's
Neck, where he landed with the principal part
of his forces. Unable to oppose this project,
Washington had in the mean time withdrawn
his troops from York Island, leaving a strong
garrison at the principal defence, called after
his name, for the purpose of occupying the attention of the enemy, and impeding his future
operations. The royalist general followed the
army of the Americans, and a trifling affair took
place at White Plains. But the cautious skill
of Washington baffled every attempt to bring
on a general action, and early in November
Lord Howe broke up his posts in this quarter
and turned suddenly towards York Island again.
Fort Washington was immediately invested at
four different points, and being nothing more

than an embankment of earth, was surrendered after a sharp but short resistance. The prisoners taken here amounted to three thousand.

Thus the republican army was daily diminishing, while that of the royalists had been increased by a reinforcement of five thousand Hessians and Waldeckers, hired by the British ministry to assist in subduing the posterity of Britons. Washington passed his army over into New-Jersey, leaving the royalists entire masters in New-York. Terror and dismay overspread the whole land. The tories every day grew more bold and insolent; the whigs began to despair of their cause; the neutrals turned partisans against their country, and the British general became arrogant with success.

His conduct towards the prisoners taken on Long Island and at Fort Washington was still more unfeeling and insulting than that of General Gage at Boston. Colonel Rawlings and some other wounded officers captured in Fort Washington were paraded through the streets of New-York on a cart, amid the jeerings of the royalists, and set down at a deserted building of a character it would be indecent to name. The allowance to the prisoners was scanty and of inferior quality. They were confined during the winter in churches and sugar-houses, where great numbers perished miserably by cold, unwholesome food, and all the indignities which pride, arrogance, and unfeeling avarice could heap on them. No means of cleanliness were allowed them; none were within the reach of their own resources, and they died in the midst of filth, the victims of oppression.

In after times these receptacles were exchanged for hospital and prison ships, anchored at the Wallabout in the East River. These were slaughter houses, where a large portion of the captives were carried only to die. Confined between decks, in the filthy caverns of these old "floating hells," as they were aptly called, as close as they could lay, and destitute of the comforts of life or the consolations of sympathy; exposed to insult and ribaldry; themselves, their country, and their cause denounced by every epithet that could add the bitterness of passion to the agonies of despair, they suffered until death, instead of coming as the king of terrors, approached as a smiling deliverer.

Complaints were answered by curses, and groans by sneers, laughter, and sometimes blows. In the hot weather they were roasted, as in an oven in the holds of the vessels, whose uncalked decks let in the rain upon their uncovered bodies; in the winter they could only keep themselves warm by twisting their emaciated limbs together. Petty and unfeeling tyrants were placed over them, as if to mock their miseries and answer their complaints by stripes and curses. Deprived thus of air, of pure water, and of wholesome food; destitute of the friends which misery so often procures even among enemies; agonizing under the present, and hopeless of the future, thousands of patriotic spirits, that deserved a better fate, died and were buried, and forgotten by their country, which at this moment cannot tell their names. Some perished of the scurvy; many of putrid fevers engendered in these dens of misery; some died of despair, and others raving mad.

These examples of suffering humanity on one hand, and arrogant, unfeeling cruelty on the other, are recorded not for the purpose of awakening the slumbering passion of revenge, or perpetuating national antipathies. I have a better and a higher motive. I wish to impress on the minds of my youthful readers an idea of the vast value of liberty by showing the price at which it was purchased, in order that they may never do any thing to forfeit the blessing. I desire also to place before them, in words as strong as I can command, the sufferings, the patience, the fortitude, and patriotism of their fathers who won and transmitted that blessing to their posterity; in order that they may never, through ignorance, be guilty of the sin of ingratitude. When they shall learn, that in the midst of horrors and sufferings not one of these firm and virtuous patriots purchased relief from his miseries by abandoning or betraying the holy cause of liberty, they will then know better how to estimate their fathers, and tread in their steps, should it ever be necessary to make similar sacrifices. The name of Arnold stands alone in a dreary and infamous solitude, as the only one that stained the annals of a glorious contest by betraying his country.

If this treatment of his prisoners arose from bad feeling on the part of General Howe, it was as cruel as impolitic. So far from quelling the obstinacy of resistance, it added new vigour to its action, and imparted the energies of revenge to the desire of freedom. The spirit which is not crushed by oppression becomes invincible.

But it was not merely the prisoners that were treated in this unmanly and shameful manner When General Howe passed into New-Jersey in pursuit of Washington, the inhabitants remained for the most part quietly at home, under the sanction of protections that were perpetually violated. The Hessians could not read English, and if they had been able, would have paid little attention to them. They had been told by those who sold, as well as by those who bought them, that they were going to fight against savages, who spared neither sex nor age; who were the enemies, not only of all governments, but of the social state, and, in short, of the whole human race. They came under this impression, and for a while acted accordingly. They however at length discovered their mistake. They found they were warring against men and Christians. When taken prisoners they were treated with a kindness they

little deserved : by degrees they became ac
quainted with the real nature of a quarrel in
which the whole human race might feel an equal
interest, for our cause was that of mankind ; and
long before the conclusion of the war, such was
their proneness to desertion, that the royalist generals did not dare to employ them as sentinels.

Such, however, was not their conduct at the
commencement of the struggle.   They rioted in
unrestrained licentiousness among the people
of New-Jersey ; property was wantonly destroyed where it could not be consumed or carried away ;   the hen-roosts were robbed ;
hogs, sheep, cattle, and poultry carried off ;
peaceable men murdered or led away prisoners ; women insulted, abused, and outraged by
every species of wantonness, and a scene of
affliction and endurance was exhibited, as dis-
graceful to one party as it was grievous to the
other.   But nothing is more true, than that the
offences of men are revenged by their own
consequences.   This course, instead of quelling the spirit of resistance, only served to give
it a new and more determined impulse.   The
thrifty and elastic sapling which was thus attempted to be pulled down to the earth and

broken, recoiled with accelerated force, and swung the assailants sky-high in the air. The Jersey Blues were not to be subjugated by insult and aggression. From that period they sought no protection but the arms of freemen The royalist general had only the satisfaction of making inveterate enemies where perhaps he might have made grateful friends, or at least conciliated a quiet neutrality. The Jersey farmers flew to arms, associated in independent parties, which finally acted in conjunction with each other, and rallying their combined force, hemmed in the royalist army to such purpose that they no longer ventured forth except in large force. Even then they were greatly harassed, and often suffered serious loss. So much for attempting to subdue a spirited people by insults and injuries.

The behaviour of the militia on Long Island, at Fort Washington, and on subsequent occasions, had very much weakened the confidence of Washington, in the possibility of sustaining the contest, without a large accession of regular troops. He had addressed a most serious remonstrance to Congress, urging this subject on its consideration, and strenuously insisting on the necessity of promptly attending to the increasing wants of the army. "I ask pardon," he says, in conclusion, "for taking up so much of their time with my opinions : but I should betray that trust which they and my country have reposed in me, were I to be silent on matters so exceedingly interesting."

The ancestors of those who were now contending for that freedom which they had sought in the wilderness of the New World had ever cherished a decided antipathy to great standing armies. They considered them, and most justly, as chosen instruments in the hands of ambitious leaders for overturning the liberties of mankind. They believed that hireling soldiers had for the most part neither patriotism nor integrity, and that they were just as likely to turn their swords against the bosom of their country as to defend it against the aggressions of others. History and experience had established the truth of this opinion, and the stern republicans of that unequalled body, the first American Congress, did not relish the idea of authorizing a power which might in the end supercede their own, and after assisting to destroy one despotism, end by establishing another. On the great general principle they were right, and no blame ought to attach to them for their unwillingness to give up their dependence on the militia. Until convinced by experience of the necessity of resorting to some other means of defence, they were perfectly justifiable in relying in a great measure on this. The greatest, and the most dangerous enemy to liberty, is a popular general at the head of a victorious army; and where there is one Washington standing alone in modern history, there are crowds of traitors who only freed their country from foreign chains to fetter it more firmly with their own.

But for the virtuous forbearance and devoted patriotism of Washington who shall say, that at the conclusion of the war, when the prize was actually gained, the apprehensions of the friends of freedom might not have been realized in the camp at Newburgh. Those, therefore, who so freely censure the conduct of as wise and as patriotic an assemblage as perhaps ever met together either in the Old or the New World for hesitating to comply with the requisitions of Washington for a great increase of the regular army, will do well to revcrence their scruples, rather than blame their delays. Both were right, and both acted in conformity with their respective situations. The one was charged with asserting the independence of his country by arms; the other with sustaining the principles of civil liberty, by a wise and salutary caution not to endanger the one in securing the other. The people of the United States might have become jealous of their Congress, jealous of their general, impatient of supporting a great standing army, and sought, by returning to their old masters, a refuge from the exactions of the new. Exercising, as it did, a precarious authority, founded entirely on the voluntary submission of the people, Congress was right to refrain from any measures that might have produced disaffection or disunion. There were always enough malcontents, and it would have been dangerous to increase their numbers.

Notwithstanding all that has been said on the subject, an armed nation, animated by the spirit of freedom, is the best defence of a country. Where that high duty is exclusively committed to a standing army, the people gradually accustom themselves to rely on it solely

They become listless and indifferent; they imperceptibly lose every vestige of public spirit, and degenerate into habits which render them both unwilling and unable to defend their own rights, or vindicate those of their country. Those who remember the battles of Lexington and Bunker Hill, the exploits of Marion in South Carolina, and, above all, the memorable victory of New-Orleans, ought not to despise militia. Strict discipline converts reasoning beings into mere machines, and it is better to depend on men, than machinery, for the defence of a nation.

After the defeat on Long Island, and the capture of Fort Washington, the cause of freedom seemed all but desperate. It is impossible to contemplate the situation of affairs at that time, without being convinced that, under Providence, the chief dependence of the states was on Washington alone. Had he despaired —had he faltered—had he remitted his exertions, his caution, his celerity, or his duty, all might, and probably would, have been lost. But he never for a moment sunk under the burden of his country. Relying on the goodness of his cause, the support of the Great Author of all good, the spirit and patriotism of his countrymen, and, without doubt, sustained by a noble consciousness of his own capacity to guide the state over this stormy ocean, he never lost sight of the port for which he was steering. He always saw the light ahead, and steered for it with a steady eye and determined hand.

He bowed his lofty spirit, which ever prompted him to meet, rather than avoid, his enemy, to stern necessity, and retreated as he advanced. New-Jersey, which soon after witnessed and shared in his triumphs, now saw him avoiding and baffling, with matchless dexterity and caution, a superior force, with which it would have been madness to contend. To add to his difficulties, disaffection began to rear its head among those who had hitherto remained quiet, and the royalists of the county of Monmouth, encouraged by the aspect of affairs, were preparing to rise in behalf of the invader.

Still Washington preserved his equanimity. Both his head and his heart remained true, and wherever opportunity offered, he faced his enemy, to retard, if he could not arrest, his career

While the British poured on with increasing numbers and confidence, his own little destitute army daily decreased. As fast as their short periods of service expired, the levies departed for their homes, leaving their general destitute of almost every means of opposition. The tories of New-Jersey became more bold with the certainty of success, and the well-affected to the cause of liberty were repressed by the presence of their enemies.

After vainly attempting to oppose the royal army, now commanded by the active Cornwallis, at Brunswick, Washington retreated to Trenton, where he resolved to remain till the last moment, having first passed his baggage and stores to the other side of the Delaware. He wished to accustom his troops to the sight of the enemy, and hoped that in the arrogance of success, Cornwallis might afford him an opportunity of striking a blow. At this moment, his cavalry consisted of a single corps of Connecticut militia; he was almost destitute of artillery; and his army amounted to but three thousand men. One-third of these consisted of New-Jersey militia, and of the others, the term of service of many was about to expire.

Add to this, the almost entire want of every thing that constitutes the efficiency of an army, and my young readers will think that the cause of liberty hung by a single hair. But it was not so. It had right and Providence on its side, and it was sustained by Washington. Supported and animated by these, a handful of barefooted soldiers, marching on the frozen ground of an American winter, and tracked by their enemies by their blood on the snow, achieved miracles, and saved their country.

General Howe, encouraged by a hope that the almost desperate aspect of affairs might now enforce his promises of pardon, issued a proclamation, offering the boon to all who, within sixty days, appeared before officers of his appointment, and signified their submission to the royal authority. Despairing of the cause, or perhaps secretly disaffected, many availed themselves of this amnesty, and a general opinion, which daily gained ground, prevailed among all classes, that a longer contest for independence was not only hopeless, but impossible. But the maxim of virtue and wisdom is never to despair. The crisis of the fever is not **always** death, and the last hour of suffering **is** often the period of renovation. Light succeeds darkness, just as surely as darkness succeeds light. Washington never despaired. While in the full tide of retreat, General Reed is said to have exclaimed, "My God! General Washington, how long shall we fly?" "Why, sir," replied Washington, "we will retreat, if necessary, over every river of our country, and then over the mountains, where I will make a last stand against the enemies of my country."

The royalist generals had not yet learned the lesson of vigilance and celerity. They did not know that presumptuous delays are the forerunners of disaster, or that the American Fabius was also the American Hannibal, when occasion required. It never occurred to them that the retreating lion will sometimes turn on his pursuers when least expected. Cornwallis remained inactive at Brunswick, leaving Washington a few days of leisure, which he employed with his usual industry in making preparations for the ensuing campaign. He urged congress, he urged the governors of the different states, by every motive of patriotism, to take measures for the safety of the country, and the success of its cause; and, while stimulating others, himself set the example which he enforced by his precepts.

While the British commanders were carousing at New-York and Brunswick, and boasting the anticipated triumphs of their master; while the true lovers of liberty seemed already wrapt in the shroud of dissolution; while the last sun seemed going down on their independence, and the last blow only wanting to the ruin of their cause, some little gleams of comfort appeared. The worthy Governor Mifflin of Pennsylvania exerted himself successfully in rousing the good citizens of Philadelphia to the defence of their country. A large portion of them imbodied themselves in arms, and fifteen hundred joined Washington at Trenton. Thus reinforced, he, who never remained on the defensive except against his will, moved upon Princeton in a direction towards the enemy then at Brunswick. On his way, however, learning that Cornwallis, having received large reinforcements, was advancing by different routes with a view to gain his rear, and cut him off from the Delaware, he changed his purpose and crossed to the west bank of the river, so opportunely that the enemy came in sight at the moment.

The two armies now remained opposite each other on the different banks of the river. The object of Cornwallis was to cross over, and either force Washington to fight him, or, in the event of his retreating, gain possession of Philadelphia. That of the American general was to prevent the enemy crossing the Delaware. For this purpose he resorted to every means in his power, slender as they were. While thus situated, General Charles Lee, who had been repeatedly urged by Washington to join him as speedily as possible with the troops under his orders, but who had wilfully delayed from time to time, suffered himself to be surprised at his quarters by a detachment of the royal army, was taken prisoner, and for a while relieved the cause of America from the mischiefs of his services. The event, however, seemed still further to depress the hopes of the Americans, already reduced to the verge of despair.

At this moment the British force on the Delaware consisted of four thousand men quartered at Trenton and the neighbouring towns. Other bodies of troops were at Princeton, Brunswick, Elizabethtown and Hackensack. Thus a large portion of New-Jersey was in possession of the enemy. The invading army, to use the words of Washington, was increasing like a snowball, by the arrival of new reinforcements and the accession of the disaffected, while his own force was inferior in numbers, and, as usual, deficient in all the necessary requisites for efficient action. Even these miserable elements were about dissolving. The ice would soon form in the Delaware, and the British general might avail himself of it to cross the river and take possession of Philadelphia, for there was no force capable of preventing him. Such an event, by further depressing the lingering hopes of the patriots, would increase the obstacles to recruiting his army, already almost insurmount able. It is impossible to read the letters of this great man at this period without shivering at the prospects they disclose ; and at the same time receiving a conviction that he was now the last stay of his country. Had he faltered in his purposes, or failed in his exertions, it had been all over with the republic. The dark night had come, and no one could tell when it would be morning.

In such trying moments as these, when the

fate of millions of men, and of countless millions of their posterity is at stake; when great principles are hovering on the verge of ruin, and every movement brings nearer the crisis of a nation's fate, then it is that the metal of a man is tried in the furnace, and the discovery made whether it is true gold or not. Where others sink he rises; through the darkness which hides the lamp of hope from all other eyes, he sees the beckoning light, and finds his way where others lose it for ever. Instead of despairing, he is roused to new exertion, and that which makes cowards of other men stimulates him only to more daring temerity. He perceives that there is a crisis in the affairs of nations when caution is no longer safety, and to march up to the teeth of danger the only road to success. When the case of the patient is desperate, so must be the remedy.

To such minds as that of Washington it must often have occurred that incautious men are very apt, while watching others, to expose themselves; that no force is strong when taken unprepared; and that an enemy certain of success is already half vanquished, since, in all probability, he will neglect the means to secure it. Prompted by this in spiration, and urged on by the absolute ne cessity of striking a blow that might awaken the slumbering energies, and revive the almost extinguished hopes of his country, he formed the glorious design of attacking the enemy at the moment he was lulled in the lap of security, waiting for the freezing of the river, to drive the Americans before him like flakes of snow in the wintry tempest.

Great was the design, and nobly was it executed, so far as the elements of nature would permit the exertions of man to be successful. The night was dark as pitch; the north-east wind whistled along the shores of the Delaware, laden with freezing sleet, and the broken ice came crashing down the stream in masses that, as they encountered the rocks above, shivered into fragments, with a noise that might be heard for many miles. Neither man nor beast was out that night, and the enemy on the opposite shore sought shelter in the houses of the citizens of Trenton from the howling storm. But Washington was up and doing. In the dead of the night, and amid the conflict of the mighty elements, the boats were launched on the bosom of the icy torrent, and after incredible exertions reached the opposite shore. Without waiting a moment to learn the fate of the other two divisions, which were to co-operate in this daring adventure, he dashed forward towards his destined prey, through a storm of hail and snow, that rattled in the teeth of his brave companions in arms, and the dawn of day saw him driving in the posts of the enemy at Trenton. The picket-guard had no time to fire, so impetuous and unexpected was the shock of the Americans; they retreated to where Colonel Ralle, who commanded the enemy, had drawn up his men. That officer fell mortally wounded almost at the first fire, and his troops retreated. Washington advanced rapidly upon them, throwing at the same time a detachment in their front, when, seeing themselves surrounded, they laid down their arms, and surrendered at discretion. A thousand prisoners, with their arms, and six field-pieces, were captured on this occasion, at the expense of two Americans frozen to death, two killed, and a single officer wounded. This was James Monroe, late president of that confederation which he had shed his blood to cement and preserve. Thus two men fought here together, in the same field, and in the same cause, who were destined in after-life to attain the highest station in the world. From the signal success which attended the division under Washington, there can be no reason to doubt that if the others had been able to cross the Delaware, that morning might have been rendered still more illustrious, by the total discomfiture of the whole British force at the different positions along the Delaware.

But even as it was, the result of that day's business was of vital consequence to the question of independence. Had Washington failed in the attempt, it would have cost him, and the greater portion of his division, their lives or their freedom. Had this been the case, the stream of liberty, already almost dry, would perhaps have ceased to flow any longer. There was but one Washington— there never has been but one in the world. If the Americans at this, the gloomiest period of their struggle, had lost him, Heaven only knows what might have been the consequences. The Power that watched over them might have supplied the deficiency, but without the wisdom and virtue of another Washington, I can not see how the country could have been saved, had he been lost.

But happily, the question was not to be tried. The result was that of entire success, so far as the plan could be carried into effect amid the insuperable obstacles of nature. That day was the dawning of centuries, I hope, of better days to our country. The attempt and the success of Washington astonished the British; and from that moment they began to discover that they had to deal with one in whose presence they could never sleep on their posts in safety.

History has seldom recorded an action more daringly judicious or more eminently successful than the one just related. It possesses all the characteristics of courage, enterprise, and sagacity; its conception was equally profound and masterly; the arrangements for its prosecution, the time chosen for carrying it into effect, and the manner in which it was borne out to complete success, all serve to demonstrate that the consummate prudence of Washington was combined with a courage and enterprise equally admirable, and that, had he possessed the means of exercising the latter quality, he would have crushed his enemy with even greater celerity than he avoided him. It was a great action in its conception, conduct, and consequences; and nothing is wanting but numbers to give it equal dignity with the most illustrious exploits of ancient or modern times.

With a view to animate the spirits of the people of Philadelphia, Washington made some little parade of marching his prisoners into that city, with the captured flags and cannon, and bristling bayonets. By this exhibition the disaffected were overawed, and the friends of liberty animated to new exertions.

Throughout the whole of the revolutionary war the prisoners taken from the enemy had been uniformly treated with humanity by the Americans, except in retaliation of their own conduct to ours. Those captured at Princeton consisted principally of Hessians, and if ever provocation could justify inhumanity, the excesses of these men would have furnished an excuse. Both history and tradition unite in recording almost innumerable instances of individual cruelty, insult, and robbery on their part, calculated to call forth the bitterest feelings of vengeance in the breasts of those who suffered, and those who sympathized with the sufferers. This was the first opportunity of repaying them, and the humanity of Washington retaliated their injuries by kindness. They were treated with every proper attention compatible with the means in his power, and the result proved on this, as on every occasion which occurred during the war, that humanity, like honesty, is always the best policy.

The Hessians, as I have before observed, had come over to the New World full of prejudices against the Americans. They considered them little better than savages, and treated them as if they were without the pale of civilized warfare. They were told that if taken they would receive no quarter, and, consequently, they gave none. But the kindness with which they were treated opened both their eyes and their hearts. From this time they began to be disaffected to the barbarous service in which they had been employed; their feelings became enlisted in the cause of liberty; they took every opportunity of deserting, and of all that came over, few ever returned. Those who survived, remained among us; those who came to deprive us of freedom settled down by our side in the full enjoyment of its blessings, and became a portion of our most useful citizens. Such are the peaceful triumphs of mercy and benevolence, and such the means by which the good Washington twice conquered the enemies of his country;— once by his valour, and again by his humanity.

The news of the brilliant success at Trenton roused the British commander-in-chief at New-York, who was expecting every day to hear of the capture or dispersion of the American forces. He despatched Cornwallis, who was on the point of sailing for England, but unluckily for his future reputation was detained, into New-Jersey, with a force which, in his opinion, must carry all before it. Washington had also been reinforced, and recrossing the Delaware, once more took post at Trenton. His situation here again became extremely critical. He had, with the boldness becoming in a man conscious that the great crisis of his country's fate had arrived, determined to make a winter campaign, with a view to wrest the whole of New-Jersey from the hands of the enemy. But a force vastly superior to his own was now rapidly approaching, like an impetuous torrent, to sweep him and his little army into the freezing Delaware, and the only alternatives that presented themselves were a choice of difficulties. The state of the river was such as precluded either crossing on the ice or in boats, and if he retreated in any other direction, he would be met by a superior enemy, whom he could not successfully oppose.

In this situation, he again took council from his bold and masterly genius. He resolved once more to baffle the enemy by becoming the assailant. The van of the troops under Cornwallis had now taken possession of Trenton, and the two armies had nothing but the Assumpink, a small stream, scarcely thirty yards wide, between them. Tradition has preserved the story that Sir William Erskine urged Cornwallis to an immediate attack.

"Now is the time," said he, "to make sure of Washington."

"Our troops are hungry and tired," replied the other. "He and his tatterdemalions are now in my power. They cannot escape to-night, for the ice of the Delaware will neither bear their weight, nor admit of the passage of boats. To-morrow, at break of day, I will attack them, and the rising sun shall see the end of rebellion."

"My lord," replied Sir William, "Washington will not be there at daybreak tomorrow."

The rising sun indeed saw another sight. It saw Washington at Princeton, and the British at Trenton heard the echoes of his cannon cracking amid the frosts of the wintry morning He had, after replenishing his fires to deceive the enemy, departed with his usual quiet celerity, and marched upon Princeton, where three British regiments were posted in fancied security, not dreaming of the approach of a foe. Though surprised, the enemy made a gallant defence, and he who had so long and so often been the shield of his country, now became its sword. His capacious and unerring mind again saw that another moment had come, on which hung the destinies of his beloved country. The cause of freedom now quivered on the brink of a precipice, from which, if it fell, it might never rise again.

The British force was met in full march towards Trenton. On perceiving the advanced guard of the Americans, they faced about, and repassing a small stream, advanced under cover of a wood. A short but sharp action ensued; the militia soon fled, and the small body of regulars, being far overmatched, was broken. At this critical moment, Washington came up with the corps under his command, and renewed the action. Seeing at a single glance that all was now at stake, and all would be lost by defeat, he became inspired with that sublime spirit which always most animates courage and genius in the hour of greatest peril. He snatched a standard, and calling on his soldiers to come to the rescue of their country, dashed into the midst of the enemy. His good soldiers, animated by his words, and still more by his example, backed him bravely. The valiant British cried " God save the king," and the soldiers of freedom shouted " God save George Washington :" and he did save him. After a contest as keen as the edge of their swords, the British broke, fled, and were hotly pursued. Some went in one direction, some another. A single regiment took refuge in the college, but retreated through the back-doors on the approach of the artillery, and the classic fane consecrated to learning and science, was equally consecrated to victory.

One hundred and twenty killed, and three hundred prisoners, were the tribute paid by the enemy to the genius, enterprise, and gallantry of Washington. The Americans lost sixty-three, whose names, like those of many other humble champions of freedom, are buried in their graves. The name of General Mercer, who fell early in the action, is alone bequeathed to posterity, and deserves to be remembered, though not alone. He is recorded as one of the most precious of all our martyrs to the shrine of liberty; and his loss, which was deeply mourned at the time, will be long regretted, not on his own account, but that of his country. He who expires in the arms of victory, and in defence of his liberty, lives long enough; for he has lived to leave behind him a name that will never die.

That morning, when Cornwallis opened his eyes to the dawn, the south bank of the Assumpink was as silent as the grave, and nothing but a few waning fires remained to designate the spot that was a few hours before alive with human beings.

"Where can Washington be gone?" asked the royal general. At that moment, the distant roar of cannon was heard in the direction of Princeton.

"There he is," answered Erskine, "rehearsing the tragedy of Colonel Ralle."

"By Jove! he deserves to fight in the cause of his king," cried the other.

But he was fighting in a cause far higher than that of kings. He was sustaining the cause of freedom, and the rights of his country.

Thus once more did the heart of all America throb at the news that light had come out of darkness, and hope sprung up with renewed vigour from the regions of despair. Twice had the republicans expected to hear that all was lost, and twice had they heard that victories had been snatched from a superior and hitherto triumphant foe. The genius of liberty again held up her head amid the gloom that surrounded her, and flapped her wings for joy. Her votaries, who had partaken in her despair, shared in her rejoicings, and now, for the first time since the catalogue of disasters, which, one after the other, had depressed the very souls of the stoutest advocates and defenders of freedom, did there awake in the bosoms of all a noble prophetic consciousness, that the land which had determined to be independent was capable of achieving the boon. In ten days, Washington had changed the whole aspect of affairs, and given to his country a respite, if not a deliverance.

Soon after this second victory, the enemy went into winter-quarters at Brunswick and the adjacent villages, leaving Washington master of the ground he had gained by his gallantry, wisdom, and perseverance.

CHAPTER X.

THE cessation of actual hostilities, produced by the British army entering into winter quarters, brought no relaxation to the labours of Washington. It was his fate to struggle with difficulties that had no intermission, and obstacles without end, during the greater part of seven anxious years of almost perpetual disappointments and mortifications. Always acting, and compelled to act on the defensive without the means of defence, except when compelled by inevitable necessity, he rushed back on his enemy, gave him a single blow to check his arrogance for a moment, and then bowed his spirit to the yoke of fate.

His winters were employed in pointing out and urging on Congress and the different governors of the states the adoption of such measures as experience and disasters had proved indispensable to the final success of the cause ; in soothing the feelings of his suffering soldiers, smarting under every deprivation ; in providing as far as practicable against the severity of the winter, which smote them with tenfold keenness in their destitute situation, and in preparing for another year of trial and vicissitudes. But the vigour of his mind was equal to that of his body, and both were sustained by a consciousness of right, animated by the purest flame of patriotism. That which made others despair, only braced him to new exertions ; and the burden which would have crushed a common spirit, like the ballast of a noble ship, only made him the more difficult to overset. During the whole winter he continued to harass the enemy by skirmishes and surprises.

Nor did he stand alone, the single pillar of

the state, though assuredly the keystone of the arch. That illustrious body of patriots, the first Congress in time, in talents, integrity, and patriotism that ever convened in the United States, was not behindhand in the noble strife. In the midst of defeat and disaster, when the past presented little else than a long black catalogue of woes, and the finger of the future pointed to nothing but an aggravated repetition, that body stood firm as a rock by the side of Washington. It rejected all offers of peace without independence ; it debated the great questions, embracing life and death, infamy and fame, freedom and slavery, with a temper, a firmness, and dignity which neither ancient nor modern times have equalled. The boasted Senate of Rome sat unmoved at the approach of the barbarian chief; but the members of the old Congress of the United States exerted themselves to ward off the ruin of their country, rather than submit to it like philosophers.

Limited as were their means, and still more limited their authority, they bore themselves like the true fathers of the state. They seconded the recommendations and remonstrances of Washington, with a tempered experience which taught them not to press too heavy on a people already discouraged by ill success, and impoverished by the vicissitudes of war; and with a noble patriotism which made them cautious how they interfered with the sacred rights of the citizen, in providing for the wants of the soldiers in defence of their country. They voted the enlistment of more men; they gave every aid in filling up the regiments already authorized to be raised; they conferred on Washington powers which enabled him for six months to act independently of their orders; and on all occasions, by unanimity, talent, integrity, and firmness, so conducted themselves as to merit the gratitude of all posterity. I would enumerate them one by one, but my young readers cannot look into the records of their country without seeing them shining like stars in the firmament, nor listen to the voice of their countrymen without hearing their names coupled with blessings.

The plan ultimately adopted by the royal general for the ensuing campaign was far more extensive and better arranged than that of the preceding, which had been in a great degree the result of circumstances. The design was, that General Howe, with the main body of his army, should proceed to the southward by sea, and advance with the fleet up the Delaware upon Philadelphia, which, it was supposed, must ultimately fall into the hands of the enemy. The experience of the royal general had not yet taught him that the possession of our cities was not the subjugation of the country, and their importance was much overrated. Another object was, however, connected with the invasion of Pennsylvania. It necessarily called the attention of Washington to that quarter, and in a great measure prevented him from aiding, either personally or by detachments of his army, in impeding or defeating the other portion of their plan, which was conceived with great judgment and skill. While Washington was thus employed in defending other portions of the Union from the inroads of a superior army, Burgoyne was approaching from Canada, with a powerful force, to act in conjunction with Sir Henry Clinton, who commanded a large body in New-York, in obtaining the entire command of the whole line of the Hudson River, thus separating the north and the south. Thus divided, and incapable of giving each other mutual aid, it was supposed that each would in succession fall an easy prey. Judicious as this plan might seem, t resulted in a catastrophe as little anticipated as it was decisive. The utmost stretch of human wisdom and foresight often does nothing more than weave the web of its own destruction. The current of the stream cannot be changed by swimming against it, and what Providence hath decreed, man may not gainsay. The plan of proceeding by sea to the Delaware was probably the result of the admirable caution of Washington, who had taken a strong position on the Raritan, which rendered it dangerous for General Howe to move against Philadelphia in that direction, leaving the Americans in his rear.

Washington had gone into winter-quarters at Morristown, in New-Jersey, within less than thirty miles of Brunswick, where the troops of Cornwallis were disposed, and little more from the British head-quarters in New-York. His harassed and ill-provided soldiers required repose after a campaign of unceasing fatigues, wound up by two victories, gained by men marching and fighting on the frozen ground, with scarcely a shoe to their feet.

The campaign of 1777 opened under gloomy auspices, and promised to the republican cause little else than disasters. The army of Washington was totally inadequate in numbers, discipline, and equipment, to cope with the enemy, with any prospect of success. General Howe, with twenty thousand veteran troops, was preparing to embark for the Delaware, whence he was to move on Philadelphia; while Burgoyne was approaching with about half that number, backed by hordes of savages from the north. The genius of liberty was enclosed between two fires, and once more a fatal crisis seemed approaching.

About the latter end of July, or beginning of September, General Howe, having changed his original destination, landed at the mouth of Elk River, at the head of Chesapeake Bay, and proceeded without interruption to Brandywine River. Here he was met by Washington, who was determined to make an effort to save the capital of Pennsylvania. The consequence of this meeting was a pretty severe defeat of the Americans, who retreated, and were followed by the enemy, who took possession of the city in despite of all Washington's efforts to prevent them.

It was in this battle that the name of an illustrious Frenchman first became associated with the history of our country. Lafayette, who had heard of the noble struggle going on in the New World, panted to take part in the cause of human freedom, and evading the commands of his king, came among us, and fought during nearly the whole period of the war on our side. He shed his first blood on the banks of the Brandywine, which, while it flows, will perpetuate his name. His sacrifices and services were great, and great was his reward. He associated his name with that of Washington, and shared, and will for ever share with him the gratitude of increasing millions of freemen.

But the enemy did not retain peaceable possession of Philadelphia. Washington hovered near, and wherever he was there was no peace for the invaders of his country. He watched them with unceasing vigilance; kept them in perpetual apprehension of attack, and entailed on them the necessity of being on their guard day and night. At length, seeing an opportunity favourable to his purpose, he determined to avail himself of it with his usual ardour, which was at all times equal to his caution. He was now, in consequence of various reinforcements, at the head of twenty thousand men, and determined to act on the offensive.

The British forces had been exposed, in some degree, by the mode in which they were distributed. A portion was in Philadelphia, from whence the line of encampment extended across Germantown, a long straggling village, consisting, at that time, principally of stone houses, stretching along either side of the road for nearly two miles. In this situation it appeared to Washington that the portion of the enemy at this village might be surprised and cut off, and he promptly resolved on the undertaking.

His dispositions for this purpose were made with equal caution and celerity. But the nice co-operation of the different parts of the plan, which was indispensably necessary to its success, could not be attained. At seven in the evening of the 4th of October, the Americans moved from their encampment, and just at the dawn of the morning, a division under General Sullivan encountered and drove in the outposts of the British. He was quickly followed by the main body, which immediately entered into

action, but it was more than half an hour before the left wing came up. Each of these
parties were successful in breaking the enemy:
but Lieutenant-Colonel Musgrave, with a small
body of British, having taken possession of a
strong stone house, annoyed the Americans so
much by his fire that they stopped to dislodge
him. The time lost in this attempt, which was
unsuccessful at last, was a serious disadvantage.
The ground too was difficult, and the obscurity
of the morning prevented Washington from seeing distinctly what was going forward. The
co-operation of the different parties was broken;
the delay in attacking the stone house, and various accidents, against which no foresight can
guard, impeded the success of the attack.
The enemy rallied, and became the assailants.
The brigade under General Greene, after a
sharp encounter, was broken; the right wing
faltered; the division of Wayne, in falling back
on its friends, was mistaken for their enemies,
and confusion became general. Washington,
perceiving that all hope of success was lost for
that time, reluctantly yielded to the disappointment of his sanguine hopes, and retired from
the field, which at one moment had promised

him a harvest of laurels. He retreated about twenty miles, and halted at Perkiomen Creek, where, receiving a reinforcement of Virginians, he turned back, and resumed his former position in the vicinity of Philadelphia.

The British fleet, which landed General Howe and his army at the head of Chesapeake Bay, had afterwards entered the capes of Delaware, and sailed up that river for the purpose of aiding the operations of the land forces. Various small encounters took place at Mud Fort and Red Bank, near Philadelphia, and it was in an ineffectual attempt on the latter that Count Donop was mortally wounded, and taken prisoner. He received the kindest attentions from the Americans, and a message from Washington, expressing his sympathy. These acts of magnanimous forgetfulness of injuries, it is said, overcame the dying soldier, and brought tears into his eyes. He replied to the messenger of Washington—"Tell him," said he, "that I never expect to rise from my bed ; but if I should, my first act shall be to thank him in person." He died regretting the service in which he had embarked against a people so humane : and he is one of those whose fate was lamented by his enemies.

But the means within the grasp of Washington, though directed with consummate skill and courage, were at all times insufficient to produce any result but that of partial and temporary successes. Always inferior in numbers, or in all that constitutes the efficiency of numbers, his triumphs consisted in delaying the operations of the enemy, rather than preparing the way for his own. That, during successive years of defensive war, under every circumstance of discouragement, he saved his army, and his noble cause from utter ruin, is more to his honour than gaining victories and conquering nations with superior means. The enemy at length succeeded in forcing a way for their ships up to Philadelphia, and obtaining the necessary supplies through their co-operation.

In the mean time the war raged furiously in the north and in the south. The country was bleeding at its heart and at its extremities. Burgoyne, with a victorious army, and a band of savages, advanced from Canada through Lake Champlain, and, pouring into the state of New-York, let slip all the horrors of civilized and savage warfare. That detested union of the tomahawk and scalping-knife with the cannon and the bayonet, of Christian white man and pagan red man, was once more exhibited in all its horrors. Indian warriors and Christian soldiers now fought side by side, and it seemed doubtful which claimed the pre-eminence in reckless barbarity. The one seemed to have forgotten what the other never knew—and the tragedy of Miss M'Crea will for ever attest the consequences of this infamous association of civilized arts and savage ferocity. The apology of Christians for the barbarities of their Indian allies is, that it is impossible to restrain them; but it should be recollected that those who let slip the whirlwind are responsible for its devastations, and that, to put arms in the hands of savages, who never spare, is to become an accomplice in all their atrocities.

Throughout the whole of this struggle, the policy of the British ministry, which most assuredly did not act in accordance with the feelings of the people of England towards the United States, was harsh and unfeeling, as it was weak and impolitic. There were times, and many times, during the more early periods of the war, in which the cause of liberty seemed so desperate, that its advocates might have been subdued by kindness and forbearance. But, fortunate for the fate of freedom, and for the future destiny of our country, whenever our affairs were at the lowest ebb, or whenever the British general offered the olive-branch with one hand, with the other he at the same time perpetrated additional insults and injuries. He had to do with a people who might have been conciliated by kindness, but whom barbarities could never subdue. He preferred the wind to the sun, and the consequence was, that the Americans only girded their cloaks more manfully about them.

The high hills of Vermont and New-Hampshire echoed to the groans of the blood-stained valleys of New-York, and the Green Mountain Boys, seizing their unerring rifles, rallied in the cause of their country and countrymen. The first check given to the triumphant invader was by the militia of Vermont, by those who have ever since been distinguished by the honourable title of Green Mountain Boys, though they possessed the arms and the souls of heroic men. On the memorable heights of Bennington, the Hessians were once more to feel the courage and humanity of those who, while defending their own lives, respected the lives of their most obnoxious enemies.

Here Breymen and Baum, two experienced officers who had been despatched to procure supplies of cattle and horses, and to secure or destroy a depot of provisions collected by the Americans, were met by Starke, and bitter was the greeting he gave them. Colonel Baum, failing in his first objects, fortified himself in a favourable position, and waited for his associate Breymen. Before he had time to arrive, the Green Mountain Boys rushed upon his intrenchments with such irresistible impetuosity that nothing could stand before them. The valleys rung with the roaring of cannon answered by a thousand echoes of the mountains, mingled with shouts and dying groans On the first assault the Canadians took to their heels; Baum received a mortal wound, and not a man of all his companions escaped—all were either killed or taken, and six hundred Germans totally annihilated.

Ignorant of the fate of his old comrade, Colonel Breymen came up a few hours afterwards, where he met his victorious enemies instead of conquering friends. He was received, not by the shaking hands of welcoming comrades, but by the winged messengers of death from the weapons of his foes. His troops, after sustaining a few fires from the unerring rifles of the Green Mountain Boys, broke and sought shelter in the woods, where, by degrees, they were at different times nearly all taken.

This was another crisis in the great cause of liberty. The fortunes of Burgoyne had hitherto rolled on the flood tide of uninterrupted success. But it had become high water with him, and the tide ebbed as rapidly as it had flowed, leaving him and his fortunes high and dry ashore. About the same time that the parties of Baum and Breymen were destroyed, the force co-operating with Burgoyne under Colonel St. Leger, consisting of British and Indians, being met by a fierce resistance, and alarmed by a false report, raised the siege of Fort Stanwix, an important position on the Mohawk. The Indians, discouraged by a tedious series of approaches, which resulted in a total disappointment of anticipated plunder and massacre, deserted their allies and departed to their woods; while General Gates, who com

manded the American force in the north, was
daily reinforced by brave spirits flocking from
the fields and the mountains. Arnold, who
afterwards devoted himself to never-dying infamy, was there; and Morgan, whose fame is
equally immortal, was also there with those
famous riflemen whose every shot was death
to an enemy.

The approach of Burgoyne from the north
was connected with the expected movement
of Sir Henry Clinton, with a force from the
south. They were to meet at Albany. But
one never arrived there, and the other went
against his will, since he was carried as a
prisoner, where he anticipated entering as a
conqueror.

After many severe encounters and much hard
fighting, in which Arnold, and Morgan, and
Dearborn, and Brooks, and many others I have
not space to name, distinguished themselves and
won praises from their countrymen, there was
seen a sight worth beholding. At the mouth of
the outlet of Saratoga Lake, and close to the
side of the Hudson, there lies a rich meadow,
extending a considerable distance up the stream.
It is beautiful to the eye, but far more precious

to the heart of every true lover of liberty. On the morning of the seventeenth of October, in the year 1777, on that spot was seen the first British army laying down its arms and surrendering to the soldiers of freedom—but not the last. It was one of the brightest mornings that ever opened on this New World, for it heralded the rising of the sun of freedom, which for a long while had sunk below the horizon. It was the dawn of high aspiring hopes and gallant confidence. It taught the republicans to rely on themselves, and others to rely on them. It relieved the country from an army of enemies, and it was the precursor to an army of friends. The alliance with France was the first fruits of the surrender of Burgoyne.

Smarting as the Americans were under the recollection of recent barbarities, and elevated by success, on this occasion they displayed a delicacy of feeling, a refined magnanimity, which, under all circumstances, were singularly honourable. They had faced the British in the heat of battle, in the pride of success, but they turned their backs in the hour of humiliation. When the army of Burgoyne laid down its arms in the green meadow on the bank of the

Hudson, not an American was to be seen.   Who shall say our fathers were not worthy of liberty?

The field of Saratoga will always continue to awaken in the minds of all true Americans the proudest recollections.   It is associated with an event which, more than any other that occurred during the revolutionary war, contributed to its happy termination, and carried with it a train of consequences, of which the commencement is only known, and the end can only be anticipated.   Neither the field of Marathon nor the pass of Thermopylæ possess such claims to the veneration of those who sympathize in the great cause of liberty throughout the world.   It is embalmed in its vast consequences, for the devotion of future times, and every succeeding age will only give it new interest and dignity.   No native of this land of freedom should ever pass it without pausing to contemplate the scene, and dwell for a while on the triumph achieved on this spot by the patriotism and valour of his fathers.   The noble river and the smiling meadow were its witnesses; and while the one continues its course, and the other remains green, it can never be forgotten.

CHAPTER XI.

THE army of Burgoyne consisted of about ten thousand men on leaving Canada, but was reduced to nearly one-half that number when it laid down its arms at Saratoga. At the same time that the republicans rid themselves of this formidable foe they acquired a fine train of artillery, seven thousand stand of arms, and a large quantity of military stores. Thus failed a plan which threatened the most fatal consequences to the cause of liberty, and now it was

that even the least sanguine spirits looked for
ward to ultimate success. But the boon, though
within their grasp, was not yet gained, and
Providence permitted new trials, as if to show
the value of the prize by the cost of its pur-
chase.

This great event, it was thought by Congress, would check the advance of Sir Henry
Clinton up the Hudson, and relieve General
Gates from all apprehensions from that quarter. It was therefore resolved to reinforce
Washington by drawing detachments from the
northern army. He accordingly deputed the
celebrated Hamilton, then a very young man,
acting as his aid, to urge General Gates to a
speedy compliance with the orders of Congress.

Hamilton states in a letter to Washington,
that General Gates discovered much unwilling
ness to diminish his force, and urged his apprehensions of an attack from Sir Henry Clin
ton, as a pretext for declining to furnish the
reinforcements required. There are, however,
strong reasons for believing that his conduct
originated in other motives.

It appears that an intrigue had been set on
foot to displace Washington from the command

and substitute General Gates in his place. The capture of Burgoyne, by whomsoever achieved, had carried the reputation of General Gates beyond that of any other man in the nation, with the exception of Washington, if, indeed, he was an exception; and a small party was formed in Congress, aided by a few officers, not altogether destitute of claims to distinction, to place him at the head of the armies of the United States.

How far General Gates participated in this project, whether he was an active or passive instrument, is a question which I have no disposition to discuss. Whatever may have been the real merits of this officer, and his agency in bringing about an event so auspicious to the future fortunes of the United States as the capture of Burgoyne, still, as the commanding general, who would have been held responsible for the failure of the attempt, he cannot be separated from the glory acquired by its success. His name is imbodied in history; it occupies an honourable station among the heroes of the revolution; it has become a part of the inheritance of national pride; it belongs to the people of the United States, and I would not, if I could, throw any additional shade over its brightness.

But what is already known, cannot be buried in oblivion. It is certain that he became vain of his reputation; indulged in sly inuendoes against the commander-in-chief, and seemed dissatisfied or uneasy under the burden of his glory. His whole deportment exhibited a striking contrast to the calm self-poised, self-supported dignity of Washington, who, whether in prosperity or adversity, success or defeat, sailed along in his high sphere of action, like the eagle, far above the heads of those around him, without effort or noise. You never saw the motion, or heard the flapping of his wings.

Happily for the good cause, and fortunately for the destinies of our country, the intrigue proved abortive. The army under Washington, the good people of the United States, and even the soldiers of General Gates, rejected with honest disdain the idea of a change. There was that in the character of the great Father of his Country which led confidence captive; something that, like the charmed armour of romance, blunted the sharpest weapon of calumny, and warded off the poisoned arrow. He had gained a fame which even misfortune could not injure. General Gates received the command of the force destined to act against Lord Cornwallis in the south, where his success did not justify the anticipations of his friends, or his enemies. He died at New-York, long after the revolution, and those who best knew him wondered at the caprices of fortune.

The news of the capture of Burgoyne was received in England with dismay, in France with exultation. The venerable Chatham once more raised his voice for an immediate cessation of arms, and broke forth into a strain of vehement and inspiring eloquence against the cruelty of associating savages in the warfare of civilized nations. " My lords," said he, " who is the man that, in addition to the disgraces and mischiefs of this war, has dared to authorize and associate with our arms the tomahawk and scalping-knife of the savage ? to call into civilized alliance the wild and inhuman inhabitants of the woods ? to delegate to the merciless Indian the defence of disputed rights, and to wage the horrors of his barbarous warfare against our brethren ?" But the voice of humanity, patriotism, and inspiration fell on the ears of the deaf. The ministers carried their measures by the usual majority, and corruption and vengeance triumphed for a while longer over justice as well as policy.

During the severe winter which followed the events I have related, the army of Washington, quartered at Valley Forge, in the neighbourhood of Philadelphia, suffered almost incredible hardships. Since the battle of Brandywine, they had received neither soap, vinegar, or any other articles allowed by Congress for their necessary comfort. A large portion had but a single shirt, and some none at all. Many were confined to the hospitals because they had no shoes, and between two and three thousand remained incapable of duty because " they were barefooted and otherwise naked." Their food was often insufficient, and of bad quality; and, in short, they were destitute of all those comforts which conduce to physical strength and mental power.

All this while they were within a few miles of a superior force, and without the excitement of hope; for the prospect of the future seemed but a reflection of the present. Can we wonder, my young countrymen, that these poor, naked, starving soldiers of freedom pined to return to their comfortable homes? or can we blame them if, when their term of service expired, they were unwilling to enlist again? Is it a subject of surprise or reproach that under these accumulated circumstances of discouragement and suffering, the patriotic spirit of the people almost perished under its burden, or that it became difficult to rouse and animate the militia, or inspire them with confidence? For my part, so far from censuring our fathers for their want of spirit and activity, I cannot but reverence and admire that noble firmness, which, animated by the love of liberty, resisted the pressure of such a weight of woes, and refused all offers of pardon or conciliation unaccompanied by independence. Let my young readers ponder on these things, and then ask of themselves, who shall cast the first stone at the tombs of their fathers? Let them imitate their virtues, instead of censuring their memory. May Providence grant that the posterity of these much enduring men may emulate their patriotism, and then the freedom they won for us will never be surrendered at the shrine of luxury or on the altar of fear.

The sufferings of the army, now, as on all
occasions, pierced the bosom of Washington.
In addition to this source of anguish, his proud
spirit, conscious of meriting the gratitude of his
country by every exertion of valour and of virtue, had to bear up against certain slights of
Congress, and certain censures elsewhere, that
indicated a want of confidence. Of these he
however took no notice. He had higher objects than his own feelings to demand his attention; and continued to urge on the attention of
Congress the sufferings of his poor soldiers, who
on one occasion were without a single ration.
With all the energy of true feeling, and with a
manly confidence in his own claims to be heard
and respected, he exhorted Congress to remedy
the defects of the commissary department,
where these wants principally originated; and,
with the boldness of truth, lays the blame where
it ought to rest.

"I declare," said he, in one of his letters—
"I declare, that no man, in my opinion, ever had
his measures more impeded than I have by
every department of the army. Since the
month of July we have had no assistance from
the quarter-master-general; and to want of as-

sistance from this department the commissary-general charges great part of his deficiency To this I may add, that notwithstanding it is a standing order, often repeated, that the troops shall always have two days' rations in advance, that they may be ready at any sudden call, yet scarcely any opportunity has ever offered of taking advantage of the enemy that has not been either entirely thwarted, or greatly obstructed, on that account."

Congress had fallen into the common error of inexperience, in complicating rather than simplifying the organization of the commissariat of the army. It was the fashion to establish a board for every thing, and to create a number of separate wheels, each one in some degree inde-pendent of the other, and therefore each liable to impede the action of the whole. So far was this pernicious practice carried, that, on one oc-casion, when the establishment of a whole raft of boards had been proposed by some busy-body in Congress, it is related that the late Judge Peters, of Pennsylvania, then a mem-ber, rose, and with great gravity moved that the word " board" should be expunged, and that of " shingle" inserted in its place. It is said that the amendment was fatal to the bill, and achieved what no argument could have accomplished. From that time the very mention of boards excited a smile in Congress.

Besides the privations of the army, which have been just specified, they had now to encounter a new enemy, in the depreciation of paper-money, that traitor to its country in time of danger. This depreciation, slow at first, soon acquired an accelerated motion, and, like a wheel running down hill, its speed increased in proportion as it reached the bottom. The officers and soldiers soon began to find that they were paid, if at all, in paper which was losing its value while passing from the hand to the pocket.

Experience has more than once demonstrated the ruinous consequences of a resort to the issue of paper-money on the part of a government. The mischievous facility of multiplying it; the effect that multiplication has on the prices of all the necessaries of life and the means of conducting military operations; the fluctuations in its value, arising from the increase or diminution of public confidence; and the certainty of its final depreciation, when that depreciation will surely be most pernicious to the interests of the public and to individuals, all seem to demonstrate that it is an expedient which only a stern necessity can justify. That necessity presented itself at the crisis of our revolution. The public liberty, the existence of the nation, was at stake, and the sacrifice of the future was due to the present emergency. But its consequences proved ruinous to many thousands in the end, and the catastrophe of the "continental money," as it was called, remains as an example and a warning to future generations. The extravagance of the parent, which beggars his children, is not more reprehensible than that of a government which entails its burdens on the posterity of its citizens, and thus makes them responsible for its mistakes, its ambition, and its prodigality.

In the account of his expenditures during the revolutionary war, presented by Washington to the auditor-general of the United States, there is exhibited a curious scale of the progress in the depreciation of paper money, according to the rates from time to time established by Congress, which vainly attempted to regulate this impracticable medium. From the beginning of the year 1777, when it was first issued, it remained at par value, and was equal to silver and gold until the October following, when it began to depreciate, at first slowly, then more rapidly. At the close of the following year two thousand paper dollars were worth three hundred and fourteen in specie; in November, 1780, one thousand paper dollars were worth twenty-five in specie; in May, 1781, twenty thousand paper dollars were worth five hundred in specie; and by the end of that year they were worth nothing. The confidence of the people in the government and in each other was universally shaken; the idea of having been deceived by their rulers produced resentment and disaffection; the ignorant and confiding became the dupes of the wary and unprincipled; hundreds of thousands of citizens were reduced to beggary; and thus the miseries of want were added to the evils of war.

Yet still, notwithstanding these appalling difficulties, Washington did not for a moment remit his exertions. Being authorized by a resolution of Congress, he directed that all the provisions within twenty miles of his camp should

be seized for the use of his army. The expe
dient procured a temporary supply, but was soon
rendered inoperative by the farmers concealing
their products, and pleading entire poverty.

There are points beyond which human na
ture cannot be safely pushed A single individual may be found willing to give away all to
his country, but such sacrifices cannot be expected from whole communities.

In spite of these accumulated obstacles,
Washington opened the campaign with his
usual activity. General Howe, either ignorant
of the deplorable state of the republican army,
too cautious in his movements, or perhaps overawed by the superior genius of Washington, and
recollecting that while storming his camp at
Valley Forge he might be marching into Philadelphia, neglected to take advantage of the present state of affairs. By so doing he lost an opportunity which never afterwards presented itself to him or his successors. The events which
immediately followed the opening of the campaign of 1778, not being either striking or decisive, will be passed over, especially as Washington was not personally engaged in them.

The proceedings of the British parliament

now became exceedingly interesting. Not long after the rejection of Lord Chatham's motion for a suspension of arms between England and the United States, and a like fate of others of a similar nature, the British minister, Lord North, himself brought forward a plan of pacification, which was adopted by a great majority. Before, however, the preliminary steps could be taken, the news arrived in England of a treaty of alliance having been concluded between the United States and France. The propositions were in consequence hurried off to America in the hope of preceding the arrival of the treaty.

Washington received the bill of pacification, and immediately forwarded it to Congress, with a letter expressing his fears of its consequences, if the conditions became known to the people. The propositions of the British government were referred to a committee, which made an able and spirited report on the subject, and exposed, with the keenest analysis, its unsatisfactory, insidious, and insulting provisions. The propositions of parliament, and the report of the committee of Congress, were both pub lished Soon after this occurred, a French frigate arrived having on board Mr. Deane, bearing the treaty between the United States and the French king. This event was hailed with joy throughout the whole country, as the prelude of a certain successful issue to the cause of independence.

General Howe had now taken his departure for England, whither he carried with him but little glory. He was an experienced officer in European tactics, but wanted energy, enterprise, and activity, and was utterly unable to cope with Washington, who, if he had possessed the means which the former commanded, would have quickly annihilated him.

General Charles Lee, who had more wit than discretion, thus describes Howe in a letter to Dr. Rush:—"He is the most indolent of mortals. He never took further pains to examine the merits or demerits of the cause in which he was engaged, than merely to recollect that Great Britain was said to be the mother country; George the Third, King of Great Britain; that parliament was called the representative of Great Britain; that the king and parliament formed the supreme power; that supreme power is absolute and uncontrollable;

that all resistance must consequently be rebellion; and, above all, that he was a soldier, and bound to obey in all cases whatever.

"These are his notions, and this is his logic. But through these absurdities I could distinguish, when he was left to himself, rays of friendship and good-nature breaking out. It is true he was seldom left to himself; for never poor mortal, thrust into high station, was surrounded by such fools and scoundrels. I believe he scarcely ever read the letters he signed. You will hardly believe it, but I assure you it is a fact that he never read the curious proclamation issued at the head of Elk, till three days after it was published. You will say I am drawing my friend Howe in caricature; but this is his real character. He is naturally good humoured and complacent, but illiterate and indolent to the last degree, unless as an executive soldier, in which capacity he is all fire and activity, brave and cool as Julius Cæsar. His understanding is rather good than otherwise, but was totally confounded and stupified by the immensity of the task imposed upon him. He shut his eyes, fought his battles, drank his bottle, advised with his counsellors, received orders from North and Germaine, one more absurd than the other, took Galloway's opinion, shut his eyes, fought again, and is now, I suppose, to be called to account for acting according to his instructions."

He was succeeded in his command by Sir Henry Clinton, also an officer of experience and reputation. But none ever gained lasting laurels at the expense of Washington, and least of all, Sir Henry Clinton. The alliance with France, and its anticipated consequences, rendered an entire change of measures necessary on the part of the enemy, and the new commander prepared to evacuate Philadelphia, with a view to concentrating his force at New-York.

This design was executed, and the enemy marched through New-Jersey with Washington hanging on his rear, eager to strike a blow. He had so long been harassed by the necessity of perpetually retreating, that the idea of pursuit animated him to new exertions and new vigour. At length the lion had turned on his pursuers, and almost for the first time since he assumed the command, could Washington indulge the bias of his temper, which ever prompted him to decisive action. His caution was the result of judgment and necessity, and every backward step he took was like bending the bow the wrong way. It went against the grain.

Now, however, the tables were somewhat turned. Though still actually inferior in force, he was equal in numbers, and hoped most ardently that Sir Henry Clinton would afford him an opportunity of attacking him in his march through New-Jersey. He proposed the question to a council of officers, where it was strenuously opposed by Steuben, Du Portail, and General Lee. But this did not deter him, and he resolved that the enemy should not escape without a blow, if an opening for striking it occurred. That opportunity soon presented itself, and was seized with avidity.

The march of Sir Henry Clinton was directed towards Middletown, from whence he intended to embark his army for New-York, and had now arrived at Monmouth, a small town situated on high ground, not far distant from the bay of Amboy, and presenting a strong position. Another day's march would bring him to the heights of Middletown, where he would be un-

assailable. This, then, was the last opportu
nity that might present itself, and Washington
determined to avail himself of it in despite of
the opinions of the council of officers.

Accordingly he made his dispositions for
an attack the moment Sir Henry Clinton
moved from the high ground at Monmouth,
and General Lee was directed to assault his
rear, while the remainder of the republican
army opposed him on his flanks.

The twenty-eighth of June, the day on which
this battle was fought, was intensely hot. There
was not a breath of air stirring, and the sun
shone out without a cloud, making the bayonets
and musket-barrels glitter in the eyes of the
opposing hosts. The domestic herds had retired into the shade, and every animal except
man sought shelter from the burning heat.
The panting soldiers could hardly bear up
against the burden of their arms, and the horses
that drew the artillery were in a foam. The
very birds forgot to sing their songs that morning.

At the dawn of day the army of the enemy
had taken up its line of march towards the
heights of Middletown, and left the strong po-

sition at Monmouth. Washington, hearing a
firing, presumed that Lee was now engaged,
and came rushing on to second him, when, to
his utter astonishment, he found that officer in
full retreat.

"In the name of God, General Lee, what
has caused this ill-timed prudence?" said Washington.

"I know no man blessed with a larger por
tion of that rascally virtue than your excellency," retorted Lee, sarcastically.

Washington rode on furiously, for now, for
once in his life, ill-conduct, aggravated by insolence, had conquered his equanimity. He
called to his men, and they answered his call
with three gallant cheers. He ordered them
to charge the enemy, and they obeyed without
hesitating a moment. The royalists attempted
to turn his flank, but were manfully repulsed.
They turned in another direction, and met the
valiant, steady Greene, who drove them back
with his cannon, while on the instant, Wayne,
at the head of his legion, gave them such a severe and well-directed fire, that they ceased to
act on the offensive, and took post in their
stronghold once more. The extreme heat of

the day, together with their exertions in the fight, had exhausted the vigour of both parties; some died of mere fatigue, and others fell victims to their eagerness to allay their burning thirst with cold water. Washington ordered his soldiers to be prepared for renewing the action early in the morning; but when that came, he found that the British had decamped in the silence of the night, and were now so far on their way to Middletown Heights as to destroy all hopes of overtaking them, or preventing their embarkation.

On no occasion during the whole course of the war, did Washington appear greater than at the battle of Monmouth. The extraordinary retreat of Lee, and his subsequent insolence, had roused him to the highest point of energy and awakened all the heroism of his character. He animated his troops by his voice; he inspired them by his actions, and infused the magnanimity of his own soul into the souls of his gallant troops. He exposed himself to every danger of the day, and seemed determined to make up by his own exertions for the misconduct of the arrogant Lee. One* who always

* Lafayette.

fought by his side, when higher duties did not call him away, has since borne testimony that the spirit which animated, and the genius which directed, the successful operations of this gallant battle was that of Washington. Greene, Wayne, Morgan, and many others distinguished themselves highly on this occasion, and richly merit to share with him the honours of that day. They were the well-tempered weapons, but his was the soul that directed them. The enemy claimed the victory on this occasion; but a victory succeeded by a midnight retreat is hardly worth contesting.

The republican army was indignant at the conduct of Lee, and his disrespect, to give it its mildest name, to their beloved chief called forth a burst of feeling in behalf of his insulted dignity and virtue. Washington, however, was silent on the subject. He was aware of the mischiefs arising from factions in an army, and probably expected an apology or explanation from the offender. But the subsequent steps taken by Lee precluded all further forbearance. He received a letter from that officer, couched in the most haughty and supercilious terms, and demanding reparation for "the very sin-

gular expressions" made use of by Washington
on the occasion to which I have referred.   To
this a reply was sent, assuring him that, if he
felt himself aggrieved, he should soon have an
opportunity of vindicating his conduct before a
court martial.   He was accordingly tried shortly
after for disobedience of orders, for misbeha-
viour before the enemy, and for disrespect to
the commander-in-chief.   The sentence of the
court suspended him from duty for one year,
and was unanimously approved by Congress.
This terminated his military career.   He retired to his estate in Berkeley county, Virginia,
where he lived a few years of folly and eccen-
tricity, and finally, at Philadelphia, closed a life
which he might have made useful by his
talents, had they been directed by the steadiness, prudence, and wisdom of Washington.

General Charles Lee was a native of Ches-
ter county in England, and descended from an
ancient family of that name.   He entered the
British service, commanded a company of
grenadiers at Ticonderoga in the old French
war, where he was shot through the body.   He
afterwards served in Portugal under General
Burgoyne, and subsequently in the Polish army

where he was at the period of the passage of the stamp act. He then returned to England, and used all his influence in behalf of the colonies. Shortly before the commencement of hostilities he arrived at New-York, and enlisted himself among the most ardent of the whigs. After visiting all the large cities, and making himself known to the principal political leaders by his ardour and eloquence in the cause of liberty, he purchased a plantation in Berkeley county, Virginia, near his old friend Horatio Gates, with whom he had served in days of yore.

One of the worst consequences of the colonial state is, the feeling and habit of inferiority which it never fails to produce on the part of the colonists. Treated, as they always are, by the mother country with arrogant superciliousness, or stern unkindness; deprived of all the privileges of equality; accustomed to see every day instances of preference towards the natives of the parent state, and to submit to their assumptions of superiority, they gradually acquire a dependent feeling, and in time acquiesce in a degrading distinction, which overawes their spirit, and depresses their genius.

This was, in a great degree, the state of the public mind at the period when the people of the United Colonies felt themselves called upon to accept the alternative of submission or resistance. They cherished exaggerated ideas of European, and most especially British, superiority; and when it became necessary to take up arms in defence of their rights, to have served in the British army was the great recommendation to rank and honours. Hence, while Greene, Wayne, Morgan, and many others on whom nature had bestowed the talents for command, entered the service as inferior officers, such men as Gates and Lee were appointed to the highest stations in the army, without doubt because they were born in England, and had borne a British commission. With the exception of Washington, it was thought next to impossible to find a native of the colonies capable of directing extensive military operations; and the history of our revolution sufficiently exemplifies the existence of this sentiment, in the all but successful intrigue to place General Gates in a situation for which he was greatly disqualified, and where his incapacity would in all probability have ruined our cause.

This feeling of inferiority depressed the energies and discouraged the efforts of the Americans during the whole struggle for liberty. It damped their ardour, and checked their enterprise; it weakened their confidence in themselves, and at all times operated as a nightmare upon their visions of success. It outlived the era of Independence, and it lives still, though with diminished, and gradually diminishing vigour. It no longer, indeed, plays the political tyrant; but it sways our opinions, insinuates itself into our social habits, influences our tastes, dress, and modes of living, and having resigned as prime minister of American affairs, continues still to govern by a sort of back-stairs influence. I hope my youthful readers, who form the rising hope of their country, will live to see her emancipated from this last and strongest thraldom, and that they themselves will not only assist at its funeral, but give it the death-blow. It is time that the people of the United States, who have long boasted of their superiority should at least begin to feel that they are equal to other nations.

This colonial prejudice operated in favour of Lee. He was offered and accepted the rank of major-general. Lee talked well, and wrote with a keen, sarcastic vigour, which is often mistaken for a capacity to perform great actions. But he never distinguished himself in the cause of freedom. He blamed Washington, he blamed Congress, and he blamed everybody; but he did nothing himself. When called upon by the commander-in-chief to march to his assistance at Trenton, in the darkest hour of peril, he delayed under various pretexts, and at length suffered himself to be surprised and taken prisoner, in a manner that excited the contempt of his enemies, and the laughter of his friends. It was suspected, and on grounds by no means destitute of probability, that he wished to ruin Washington in order to succeed him. His conduct at the battle of Monmouth seemed to corroborate the suspicion, and without doubt operated on the court martial to suspend him from service. His example furnishes a salutary warning against premature confidence, as well as a decisive proof that experience in one mode of warfare is only an obstacle to success in a new service and a new world. Without doubt La Fayette, Montgomery, Kosciusko, De Kalb Steuben, Pulaski, and various others of less dis unction, performed important services to our cause, and aided in purchasing for us the blessings of liberty. They merit the lasting gratitude of the people of the United States, as well for what they did, as what they were anxious to do; and they enjoy, in this new world, a reputation which amply repays them for all the services they ever rendered. Still, however, the best trust of a nation is in its own children, its own experience, and its own homebred energies. Foreign aid may assist in attaining to independence, but it cannot be preserved, except by ourselves. It was, perhaps, fortunate for the United States that European policy and national rivalry were sufficiently strong to overcome the temptation to make them pay dear for he aid they received, and save them from the general fate of all those who call to their assistance an auxiliary more powerful than themselves.

END OF VOL. I.